THEY WERE EXPENDABLE

THEY WERE EXPENDABLE

W. L. WHITE

BLUEJACKET BOOKS

NAVAL INSTITUTE PRESS
Annapolis, Maryland

Published by arrangement with Harcourt Brace & Company
First Bluejacket Books printing, 1998

Library of Congress Cataloging-in-Publication Data

White, William Lindsay, 1900–1973.
    They were expendable / W.L. White.
        p.   cm. — (Bluejacket books)
    ISBN 978-1-55750-948-2 (alk. paper)
    1. White, William Lindsay, 1900–1973.   2. World War, 1939–1945—
Personal narratives, American.   3. United States. Navy. Motor
Torpedo Boat Squadron 3.   4. World War, 1939–1945—Campaigns—
Philippines.   I. Title.   II. Series.
D811.W45   1998
940.54′25—dc21   98-13807

Printed in the United States of America on acid-free paper ♾

15 14 13 12 11   10 9 8 7 6 5

FOREWORD

THIS story was told me largely in the officers' quarters of the Motor Torpedo Boat Station at Melville, Rhode Island, by four young officers of MTB Squadron 3, who were all that was left of the squadron which proudly sailed for the Philippines last summer. A fifth officer, Lieutenant Henry J. Brantingham, has since arrived from Australia.

These men had been singled out from the multitude for return to America because General MacArthur believed that the MTB's had proved their worth in warfare, and hoped that these officers could bring back to America their actual battle experience, by which trainees could benefit.

Their Squadron Commander, Lieutenant John Bulkeley (now Lieutenant-Commander) of course needs no introduction, as he is already a national hero for his part in bringing MacArthur out of Bataan. But because the navy was then keeping him so busy fulfilling his obligations as a national hero,

Bulkeley had to delegate to Lieutenant Robert
Bolling Kelly a major part of the task of rounding
out the narrative. I think the reader will agree that
the choice was wise, for Lieutenant Kelly, in addition to being a brave and competent naval officer,
has a sense of narrative and a keen eye for signifi-
cant detail, two attributes which may never help
him in battle but which were of great value to this
book. Ensigns Anthony Akers and George E. Cox,
Jr., also contributed much vivid detail.

As a result, I found when I had finished that I
had not just the adventure story of a single squadron, but in the background the whole tragic pano-
rama of the Philippine campaign—America's little
Dunkirk.

We are a democracy, running a war. If our mis-
takes are concealed from us, they can never be cor-
rected. Facts are frequently and properly withheld
in a war, because the enemy would take advantage
of our weaknesses if he knew them. But this story
now can safely be told because the sad chapter is
ended. The Japanese know just how inadequate
our equipment was, because they destroyed or captured practically all of it.

FOREWORD

I have been wandering in and out of wars since 1939, and many times before have I seen the sad young men come out of battle—come with the whistle of flying steel and the rumble of falling walls still in their ears, come out to the fat, well-fed cities behind the lines, where the complacent citizens always choose from the newsstands those papers whose headlines proclaim every skirmish as a magnificent victory.

And through those plump cities the sad young men back from battle wander as strangers in a strange land, talking a grim language of realism which the smug citizenry doesn't understand, trying to tell of a tragedy which few enjoy hearing.

These four sad young men differ from those I have talked to in Europe only in that they are Americans, and the tragedy they bear witness to is our own failure, and the smugness they struggle against is our own complacency.

W. L. WHITE

THEY WERE EXPENDABLE

THEY WERE EXPENDABLE

"YOU don't understand," said the young naval officer, "we were expendable." He was very earnest as he lolled on the bunk in the officers' quarters of the torpedo station at Newport, along with the other three officers who had also just got out of the Philippines.

I admitted I didn't understand.

"Well, it's like this. Suppose you're a sergeant machine-gunner, and your army is retreating and the enemy advancing. The captain takes you to a machine gun covering the road. 'You're to stay here and hold this position,' he tells you. 'For how long?' you ask. 'Never mind,' he answers, 'just hold it.' Then you know you're expendable. In a war, anything can be expendable—money or gasoline or equipment or most usually men. They are expending you and that machine gun to get time. They don't expect to see either one again. They expect you to stay there and spray that road with

3

steel until you're killed or captured, holding up the enemy for a few minutes or even a precious quarter of an hour.

"You know the situation—that those few minutes gained are worth the life of a man to your army. So you don't mind it until you come back here where people waste hours and days and sometimes weeks, when you've seen your friends give their lives to save minutes—"

"Look, never mind about that," said Lieutenant John Bulkeley, the senior officer. "People don't like to hear about that. I've learned that in the week I've been back. Let's start at the beginning. And first a word about us.

"We four are what is left of Motor Torpedo Boat Squadron Three. Last fall there were six little boats—and about a dozen men to a boat. Each one is a plywood speedboat, seventy feet long and twenty feet wide, powered by three Packard motors which can send her roaring over the top of the water about as fast as a Packard automobile ever gets a chance to travel on a highway. So fast, in fact, that those motors have to be changed every few hundred hours. They should be, but what happens to that pretty theory in a war is another story—we lost every spare motor when our bases were bombed, and some of those in the boats had to do quadruple their allotted term before the boats were lost—but that's getting ahead of the story.

"Each boat is armed with four torpedo tubes, and four 50-caliber machine guns—firing in pairs from each side. As for armor, well, there's a story on that. The first time we tangled with the Japs one of our machine-gunners kept crouching down behind the shield which rose just under the noses of his guns. When it was over we asked him why he hadn't stood up to fire.

" 'Hell,' he said, 'I didn't want to get nicked. I was crouching down behind that armor.' Then we had to tell him that shield was ⅜-inch plywood—keeps spray out of your eyes, but it can't stop anything the Japs might send. There isn't an ounce of armor steel on the boat—we're little eggshells, designed to roar in, let fly a Sunday punch, and then get the hell out, zigging to dodge the shells—but again I'm getting ahead.

"We went out to the islands last fall. I was com-

5

manding officer of the squadron—I'd picked every officer and man in the outfit from volunteers— told them we were heading for trouble. So they piled us and our six boats on a tanker. In late summer, we snuck through the Panama Canal one night, and were steaming up Manila Bay in the early fall.

"On my way back here last week, I had a few hours in Honolulu, and the boys were still talking about how they'd been surprised on December 7. I don't know why they should have been, because they got the same warnings we did in Manila. That war was maybe days, perhaps even only hours, away. The only thing that surprised us was that it was Pearl Harbor that got the first attack, not us.

"We'd been following the negotiations. We knew we needed sixty more days to put the islands in shape for decent defense. We needed planes and tanks. Most important of all, at least half the Filipino army had never had a uniform on until a few weeks before the fighting started. They needed training, and Washington knew this just as well as we did, and of course didn't want war.

"But now for a little geography. Here's Manila Bay—a big beautiful harbor twenty miles across. At the far end is the city of Manila, and if you were suddenly put down there, you'd think you were in Los Angeles, until you noticed the faces of the people. At the mouth of Manila Bay, the upper lip is Bataan Peninsula and the lower one is Batangas, with the Rock—Corregidor Island —a hard little pill between the two lips. And we are stationed at Cavite, the big American naval base on the lower side of the bay, about halfway between Manila and the harbor's mouth.

"We're under orders of Admiral Hart, who is Commander in Chief of the Far Eastern fleet, based there. Only how long will we stay? Because as war drew close, rumors began to fly. If it came soon, we might be getting out because we didn't have air superiority. The Japs could run down from Formosa and bag our little Asiatic fleet, so maybe we'd be pulling out for the southern islands, waiting for aircraft carriers which would bring fighters to protect us.

"The night of December 8 we were all asleep in the officers' quarters at Cavite," Bulkeley went on, "when my telephone rang about three in the morning and I first learned the Japs had struck at Pearl Harbor."

"When they shook me, I didn't believe it," said Ensign Akers. He's a tall, dark, silent Texan. "I was sure they were kidding. I just said, 'It's a hell of a time to declare war,' and rolled over."

"The message said I was to come on down to the Commandantia," continued Bulkeley. "It's an old thick-walled Spanish building, and when I got there, Admiral Rockwell, who was in command at Cavite, and Captain Ray, his chief of staff, were already dressed. Dawn was just beginning to break over Manila Bay, and the Admiral was watching the sky. 'They ought to be here any minute,' he said. And then he told me to prepare my six boats for war stations. They were going to send us over to Bataan at the naval base in Mariveles Harbor, just opposite Corregidor."

"I was prepared for the war," said Kelly, the squadron's second in command, a tall blond lieutenant with quick blue eyes. "I'd heard about the secret operation orders—what the fleet would do under any of three eventualities, so the night before I'd gone over to the Army and Navy Club at Manila and put aboard the thickest charcoal-broiled filet mignon I could buy there, plus French fries and a big tomato with Roquefort dressing, finishing off with brandy and a cigar. I figured I'd at least have them to remember.

"We spent that first day fully manned, anticipating a bombing attack. Five of the boats were dispersed along the shore about a hundred yards apart—the sixth was patrolling. All day we loaded them with food—cans of corned beef, Vienna sausage, vegetables, and canned potatoes—don't laugh at that, it's better than rice—canned fruit, fruit, coffee, whatever we could get our hands on.

"I saw the first planes about noon flying out over the bay. At first I thought they were ours, but after about a minute our shore batteries opened up. They were coming over at 20,000, and of course immediately we shoved all our boats off and out into the bay. But we heard nothing drop. It was probably just a reconnaissance raid—feeling us out.

"Of course there were all kinds of rumors—that Zamboanga and Davao, down in the southern archipelago, had been taken. Also that our navy patrol planes had gone up to Northern Luzon to intercept Jap transports gathering off Aparri there. ·We even heard our aircraft tenders had been surprised and taken, but that one proved false. Yet that morning, nothing was sure.

"About three o'clock orders came from Squadron Commander Bulkeley to send three boats, under my command, over to Mariveles on Bataan and report to the submarine tender there for food, water, and torpedoes, and to remain on the ready —available to go out and attack anything he ordered us to. By five o'clock we cast off. We had some passengers to deliver at Corregidor, so it was eight and plenty dark before we were outside the mine fields, feeling our way into Mariveles. We thought we knew those mine fields, but in pitch-darkness, with the mine-field lights turned off and of course no lights on our boats now, it was something else again

"At this point the army took over. They heard the roar of our motors and thought it was Jap planes. Searchlights began winking on all over Bataan, feeling up into the sky for planes—our motors were echoing against the mountains on Bataan, so they couldn't tell where the noise was coming from. Every artillery post for twenty-six kilometers around went on the alert, and for a few minutes it was a question whether we were going to be blown to hell by a mine or by one of our own shore batteries.

"But finally we snaked through, tied up alongside our sub tender, and then its skipper delivered a piece of nasty news. Told us he had orders to get under way just before daylight, out to sea—didn't know just where they were sending him—maybe south, maybe the Dutch East Indies, anyway he wouldn't be back.

"So then the fun began. There we were—no base, rations for only ten days, and a big problem in how we were to live ourselves and what in hell we would do with the boats when the planes came over. In addition to which, we were almost flat out of gas, and what would we do for fuel to fight this war?

"Pretty soon we began finding some of the answers. For instance, just around the coast from Mariveles in Sisiman Cove was a native village—practically abandoned except for a few families—about twenty nipa huts in all. We moved in and took over. A nipa hut is a little contraption—single room with thatched roof and sides—up off the ground four or five feet on bamboo stilts. Under it the natives keep their pigs and chickens. The floor is split bamboo, and never very tight, so the crumbs and small pieces of garbage dropped on it can sift down onto the pigs and chickens. In one corner of the hut is a sandbox, and on this sand they build a fire for cooking. There never is a chimney—the smoke just goes out the windows or through the floor cracks.

"But for the most part we lived on our boats—had to, because we never knew when we would have to haul out into the bay in case of a dive-bomber attack. Anyway we had a base again.

"Next, we found our barges loaded with gasoline in drums which had been towed out into the bay for us by the navy—if they got smacked by bombs, they didn't want them burning near the wharves. There was nobody in charge but a watchman. Each boat holds two thousand gallons, and of course it was a job pouring all that through a funnel. But in addition, it was dangerous, because our motors have to have 100 octane gasoline—airplane grade—and that volatile stuff is more ticklish than dynamite. A little bit of static can make a hell of an explosion, so usually the officers did the nasty jobs of fueling and cleaning gas tanks. No use to ask men to take risks when officers should lead.

"We noticed, as we poured, that this gas had both water and rust in it—yet there was no way to strain it out; we had no chamois. What we couldn't then know was, this gas had been sabotaged. We'll never find out when or where—the guy who did it is safe, if he's alive. But someone had dissolved wax in it—wax which congealed inside our gas tanks in a coat half an inch thick— wax which clogged our filters so that sometimes we'd have to stop and clean them after an hour's run. That's the fuel we had to fight the war on, we were to find out.

"Then I went over to the section base to make arrangements for our food, and we got another bump. The navy already realized a food shortage was coming and cut us down to two rations a day —breakfast and supper. All you got for lunch was stomach cramps about noon. There were plenty of them.

"I also thought I'd better have the doctor look at my finger. I'd snagged it a few days before and hadn't paid much attention, but now it was swollen about as thick as a walnut. I guessed maybe it was a minor strep infection. What I didn't know was that out East the streptococci are bigger and meaner than bulldogs and not to be fooled with. He took one look and began to talk about the hospital, but I said the hell with that. I was the second officer of the squadron and badly needed. I couldn't stop the war for a sore finger. Then he said I ought to go over to Corregidor, where they had some sulfa drugs. But that was out, too, because momentarily we expected to be sent out on a mission. Bulkeley had put me in charge of the three boats, and I couldn't leave.

"We settled that I'd come over to see this doctor daily, and soak it an hour or so in hot Epsom salts. The soaks, as it turned out, had to be cold because we didn't have the power for heating water, and although I saw him about every day, it so happened that whenever I got there an air-raid alarm would go off and the doctor would have to dive for a fox hole. But it was the best we could do

"The big alarm came at noon on December 10 —we'd pulled up alongside a mine sweeper for water when word came that a large flight of Jap planes was headed toward the Manila area, coming from the direction of Formosa. We pulled away from the tender, out into open water, and fifteen minutes later we saw them—several formations—I counted about twenty-seven to twenty-nine planes in each—two-motor bombers—lovely, tight, parade-ground formations, coming over at about 25,000 feet. But, I thought, when our fighters get up there and start rumpling their hair, those formations won't look so pretty. Only where were our fighters? The Japs passed on out of sight over the mountains, and then we began hearing the rumble of bombs—only first we felt the vibrations on our feet, even out there in the water, and we knew something was catching hell.

But what? Manila? Maybe Nichols Field? Or even Cavite, our own base? We couldn't know."

"I did," said Bulkeley laconically. "I was there, at Cavite. The Admiral sent us a two-hour warning that they were coming—from Formosa, and headed on down in our direction across Northern Luzon. So we hauled our boats out into the bay. They kept beautiful formations, all right. The first big V had fifty-four planes in it, and they came in at about 20,000, with their fighters on up above to protect them from ours—only ours didn't show! We couldn't figure it. First they swung over Manila and began to paste the harbor shipping. It was a beautiful clear day, and I remember the sun made rainbows on the waterspouts of their bombs. They were from a hundred and fifty to two hundred feet high, and it made a mist screen so dense you could hardly tell what was happening to the ships. It turned out nothing much was—they only hit a few.

"But then that big beautiful V pivoted slowly and moved over Cavite—began circling it like a flock of well-disciplined buzzards.

"They were too high to see the bomb bay doors

open, but we could see the stuff drop slowly, picking up speed; only as we watched we found we
had troubles of our own. Because five little dive
bombers peeled off that formation, one by one,
and started straight down for us. When they were
down to about fifteen hundred feet, they leveled
off and began unloading. Of course we gave our
boats full throttle and began circling and twisting,
both to dodge the bombs and to get a shot at them.
Our gunners loved it—it was their first crack at the
Japs. I remember Chalker's face; he's a machinist's
mate from Texarkana—a shootin' Texas boy. He
was pouring 50-caliber slugs up at them, cooler
than a pail of cracked ice, but that long, straight,
pointed jaw of his was set. Houlihan, who was
firing the other pair of 50's, was the same. They'd
picked out one plane and were pouring it up into
the sky, when we saw the plane wobble, and
pretty soon she took off down the bay, weaving
unsteadily, smoking, and all at once, two or three
miles away, she just wobbled down into the drink
with a big splash. So we know the 35 boat got
one. Meanwhile the 31 boat had shot down two
more. After that the planes didn't bother strafing

17

the MTB's. Guess the Jap pilots back at their Formosa base passed the word around.

"It certainly surprised our navy too, which had never guessed a torpedo boat could bring down an airplane. Later on I got a kidding message from Captain Ray, chief of staff:

DEAR BUCK: I REALLY THINK YOUR GANG IS GETTING TOO TOUGH. THE LATEST REPORT IS THAT "THREE DIVE BOMBERS WERE SEEN BEING CHASED OVER MARIVELES MOUNTAIN BY AN MTB." DON'T YOU THINK THIS IS CARRYING THE WAR A BIT TOO FAR?

"About 3:30 the Japs left, so we went on back in to Cavite to see what had happened. They'd flattened it—there isn't any other word. Here was the only American naval base in the Orient beyond Pearl Harbor pounded into bloody rubbish. We didn't have time then to think about where our American planes could have been, because the place was a shambles, and we began loading in the wounded to take them to Canacao hospital. The first boatload was all white Americans except one Negro—from a merchant marine boat—with a compound fracture—his shoulder bone was sticking out and it looked brick-red against his black skin. We put a tourniquet on him and never once did he whimper—a very brave guy. There was half an inch of blood on the landing platform at Canacao —we could hardly keep on our feet, for blood is as slippery as crude oil—and the aprons of the hospital attendants were so blood-spattered they looked like butchers.

"We went on back to Cavite and offered to carry more wounded. The big base was one sheet of flame except for the ammunition depot. Only a piece of the dock was left, and through the shimmering flames you could see only jagged walls. Then we saw Admiral Rockwell—he was directing the fire apparatus which was trying to save the depot. He is a tall man, a fine figure of a sailor, but his head was down that day. In a dead voice he told us we'd better get out—that the magazine was liable to go up any minute. We offered to take him with us to Mariveles, but he said no, his job was here, to do what he could to save the magazines.

"So we picked up from the gutters and streets a lot of cans of food we knew we would need—

they were from the bombed warehouses—stacked them in the boat, and set out."

"The weirdest thing I saw there," said Ensign Akers, "was a native woman—every stitch of clothing blown off by a bomb, running around screaming, completely berserk. But you could see she wasn't wounded, and so everybody was too busy to catch her and calm her down. How she got there no one knew or even asked."

"I was back there a couple of days later after the fires were out," said Ensign Cox, a good-looking yellow-haired youngster from upstate New York. "They were burying the dead—which consisted of collecting heads and arms and legs and putting them into the nearest bomb crater and shoveling debris over it. The smell was terrible. The Filipino yard workers didn't have much stomach for the job, but it had to be done and done quick because of disease. To make them work, they filled the Filipinos up with grain alcohol. The weirdest thing of all was that the week before I'd bought a bike, and the night before the raid I'd left it locked against a wall. Just for curiosity, I went over to where it had been and there it still was—beside the wall, which was only a jagged ruin, and yet its paint wasn't even scratched. I unlocked it and rode all over the yard, watching those staggering Filipinos, maybe dragging a trunk toward a crater, pulling it by its one remaining leg, or else maybe rolling a head along like over a putting green. The Japs must have killed at least a thousand. Mostly dock work- ers—they caught them right at dinner hour."

"That raid gave me my first big shock of the war," said Lieutenant Kelly, "but it wasn't the damage they did. From over in Mariveles I couldn't see what was happening after the Jap bombers disappeared over the mountain. I got my shock after they had unloaded and flew over us on their way home—the same beautiful tight for- mations—not a straggler. Where was our air force? What could it mean? Didn't we have about one hundred and fifty planes—most of them fighters? Were our guys yellow? Or had somebody gone nuts and told them not to take off—let the Japs get away with this? It made you sick to think about it.

"From over towards Cavite we could now see

21

that huge column of smoke rising into the sky as the Japs left the scene.

"But it wasn't until Lieutenant DeLong dropped in at four o'clock in the 41 boat that I knew how bad off we were. He said the Cavite base was a roaring blast furnace—the yard littered with those mangled and scorched bodies—and furthermore that all our spare parts for the MTB's—engines and everything—had been blasted to bits. Machine shops completely gone. Not so much as a gasket left to see us through this war, with the factory halfway around the world.

"Also he said the Cavite radio had been hit. That still left the short-wave voice stuff to talk with Manila or Bataan or the Rock, but of course this couldn't be secret from the Japs, so they would be depending on our six boats for courier duty to relay all confidential stuff."

"So I wasn't surprised," said Bulkeley, "when early the next morning I got a hurry call to report to the Admiral in Manila. As our 34 boat cleared the mine fields around Bataan, looking over toward Manila I saw something very queer—shipping of all descriptions was pouring out of that

Manila breakwater into the open harbor—destroyers, mine sweepers, Yangtze River gunboats, tramp steamers, all going hell for breakfast. And then I saw them—a big formation of about twenty-seven bombers. By then I was beginning to learn that if we saw planes in the air, they would be Japs, not ours. Then came another formation of twenty-nine, and still another of twenty-six.

"If they were after shipping, we shouldn't get too close to the other boats, so I changed course. They wheeled majestically around the bay's perimeter, and each time they passed Manila a load would go whistling down and presently huge columns of black and white smoke began rising—we could even see some fires, although we were still eleven miles away.

" 'Where in hell is our air force?' our crew kept asking me. 'Why in Christ's name don't they do something?'

"But the thing that really got me was that these big Jap formations, circling the bay like it was a parade maneuver, each time would sail impudently right over Corregidor! Didn't they know we had anti-aircraft guns?

"They knew all right, but it turned out they knew something I didn't. For presently all twenty of Corregidor's 3-inchers opened fire, and it made me sick to see that every one of their shells was bursting from 5,000 to 10,000 feet below that Jap formation. Those pilots were as safe as though they'd been home in bed. Later I found out what the Japs apparently already knew—that the Rock's anti-aircraft guns didn't have the range. And only then did it begin to dawn on me how completely impotent we were.

"When the Japs cleared out," continued Bulkeley, "Kelly and I headed for Manila and docked about three o'clock. When we reported, Commander Slocum told me the Admiral was considering sending our three boats on a raid off Lingayen, and were we ready? We said we were rarin' to go. So he said to stick around a couple of hours, and meanwhile to load the boats with files, records, and so forth, because they were moving headquarters. It had escaped so far, but right here on the water front it was too vulnerable—sure to get smacked. Through the open door we could see the Admiral conferring with his chief of staff and half a dozen other high officers. On the wall was a chart of the waters off Luzon, and on it black pins which represented Jap boats.

"But just then," said Kelly, "Commander Slocum looked down at my arm, which was in a sling, frowned, and said I should get over to see the fleet doctor. The doctor took off the bandage and began to talk tough. Said he couldn't do anything, and that I was to get that arm to a hospital as fast as I could.

"I was dead set on that raid, but I decided it wouldn't be tactful to bring that up, so I said, 'Aye, aye, sir,' and skipped it. We loaded the boat with records, and then went back to headquarters, where we were told that the Jap convoy off Lingayen included eight transports and at least two battleships (one of these must have been the one that Colin Kelly later got), but that we weren't going to be sent. They were saving us for 'bigger things.'

" 'My God!' my junior officer said later, 'I didn't know they came any bigger! What do they think we are?'

"Anyway the Admiral patted Bulkeley on the

shoulder and said, 'We know you boys want to get in there and fight, but there's no sense sending you on suicidal missions—just now.'

"So that was that, and we went on out across the bay, to our thatched village.

"You might call the next few days quiet for us, although my arm began giving me hell. But the only other thing was routine bombings around the bay, but from our village in Sisiman Cove we could seldom see the objective—only the massed planes returning, always unscathed.

"Presently Bulkeley dropped in on us in the 41 boat, bringing us some stuff issued by the navy to replace everything we'd lost at our quarters in Cavite—a shirt each, underdrawers, a few tubes of toothpaste, and razors—two for each boat, one for the men and one for the officers. But with each razor there were only three packages of blades, so we saw beards in the offing.

"Bulkeley had heard about my hand from a pharmacist's mate and asked me if I could stick it for two more days until he could relieve me. He himself had to be on call for consultation with the Admiral, while they needed DeLong and his boat for courier duty. I said 'sure.'

"But the next few days were hell. The whole arm began swelling, and my hand was the size of a catcher's mit. The nights were worse, because I couldn't lie down for any length of time. Also I had to keep my arm held up, or blood running down into it would drive me nuts, and it stiffened that way. The doctor at Mariveles kept offering me morphine, but I didn't dare. There might be an emergency where we'd have to get the boats out to sea quick. Bulkeley had left me in charge, and morphine might make me sleep so hard I couldn't waken for an air-raid alarm. The worst thing was the flies—they kept buzzing around trying to get into that open incision in my finger as I held my hand up in the air. And also I was running a little fever—about four degrees.

"When Bulkeley got back he took one look at me and ordered me to the hospital at Corregidor. But when we got there they told us that beautiful big modern one-thousand-bed hospital had been abandoned. There it was, I don't know how much it had cost, as useless to us as a Buddhist monastery. The patients had all been moved down into one hundred beds in one of the tunnels in the Rock. I wasn't so delirious that I couldn't figure out why. Because with no aircraft or anti-aircraft protection, that big expensive topside hospital was just an unprotected target.

"The next I remember was down in the tunnel in the army hospital under Corregidor, the army doctor asking me what treatment I'd had as he cut the shirt off my back—it wouldn't come off over my hand any more. When he found out I hadn't had any sulfa pills, he gave me a big mouthful of them to chew. He said I'd probably lose the whole arm because blood poisoning had set in solid clear to the shoulder, but he'd do what he could, and in a few minutes more I was flat on my back with my arm packed tight in hot-water bags.

"But the thing that impressed me most—even then—was the army nurses. There were fourteen of them on the Rock, and remember, I hadn't talked to a white woman since we sailed from the States. Heretofore, I hadn't paid much attention to women, but somehow the war and everything made a big difference.

28

"Or maybe it was Peggy herself, because she was a very cute kid. A brunette about medium height and very trim, but mostly it was her green eyes, I guess, and a cute way she had of telling you very firmly what you had to do, so that you grinned, but just the same you did it. She started right in bossing me around while she helped cut off my shirt.

"But don't think I didn't have competition. The Rock was built to accommodate four thousand men, but eleven thousand were already jammed in there, each of whom would have given his right ear for even a look from one of those fourteen girls. So if later on she got to like me pretty well, Peggy can't ever say she didn't have a selection to choose from. Competition was pretty stiff.

"By the time I left that hospital, I think almost all of those fourteen girls were engaged. The head nurse, Ann, a pal of Peggy's, was engaged to a major on Bataan. But he was attached to a field hospital just back of the front, so they could only write. Then Stevie—she was about twenty-seven—was engaged to an army captain in the field artillery. He'd practically followed her out there from the States. Luckily for them, he ended up in the field hospital himself, just about the time Stevie got transferred up there, so she saw him every day.

"Then there was Charlotte—she began going steady with an anti-aircraft lieutenant who was later wounded. Still another girl was engaged to the General's adjutant—a young captain.

"Because I was the only naval officer in this army hospital, I got to be a kind of pet with the nurses—I was their curiosity. Another reason might have been that I was always trying to cheer them up. The doctors were all reservists, going around with long faces, singing the blues about the way the war was going. I kept saying hell no, we weren't licked yet, and then what did they mean, the folks at home had forgotten us—of course they hadn't. Didn't they hear the radio from the States and what it was saying about our fight? I always had a cheerful angle on anything for the girls, and they began calling me their one-man morale officer."

"The whole army was listening in," said Bulkeley. "Don Bell, that Manila radio announcer who they say was shot by the Japs the first day they entered the city, was always encouraging. And even more so was KGEI from the American west coast, telling us we wouldn't be forgotten, that the people knew we were putting up a magnificent fight."

"About this time," said Kelly, "I began hearing rumors that the whole air force had been wiped out, but in the face of all this optimistic stuff, I just couldn't believe them.

"The first influx of patients we had at my hospital were survivors from the interisland steamer *Corregidor*—full of refugees, mostly natives, leaving Manila. She'd run smack into one of our own mines and sunk like a rock. I don't know whose fault. Maybe she hadn't bothered to get a chart of the mine field. Maybe the chart the army gave her was inaccurate. Anyway we could hear the explosion even in the hospital.

"It came at eleven at night," Bulkeley went on. "I had my three boats out there by 11:30. Funny thing, that old ship had been an aircraft carrier in the battle of Jutland—first boat ever to launch a plane in actual battle. She survives the whole German Imperial fleet and more than twenty years later ends up on an American mine halfway round the world.

"When we got there, survivors were so thick we didn't have to zigzag to pick them up—just went straight ahead and we got all we could handle, although there were cries coming out of the darkness all around. Finally our shoulders got so weak pulling them up the sea ladder that we couldn't lift them. So we'd throw lines out into the dark—it was like casting for trout—and haul them back with a dozen people hanging on. We'd just pull them on in—scraping off a few ears, and now and then a nose and plenty of skin, on the side of our boat—but they were drowning every minute and it was the only way. Our boat managed to rescue as many as 196. Had 'em lying and standing every place.

"The passengers themselves would help. One American, a guy called Ellis, must have saved a dozen himself. His wife was good, too. When they pulled her out, she had on only a bra and panties, so a sailor took her down to the cabin to give her dungarees. 'Come back here, young man,' she said, 'this is no time for modesty—wipe off my back!' I forgot to say there was three inches of oil on the water. After she was wiped she got to work on the first-aid squad.

"But the queerest thing came at the end. The cries out in the darkness had almost stopped, and we were cruising for the crumbs when suddenly, out over the water, I heard someone whistling—a tune! I couldn't believe it. But we changed course, and presently came alongside an aviator. He'd been blown way out there along with three life belts. He'd put one of them under his feet, another under his head like a pillow, and the third under his behind. Had his hands comfortably folded on his stomach. He thanked us, said he couldn't swim, so he'd been whistling just to kill time until someone came along. Asked if there was anything he could do. That guy had plenty guts.

"Six of the survivors died before we could land them—exposure and burns."

"They began bringing them into my hospital before dawn," said Kelly. "One of them was a Filipino boy who'd been second engineer. He'd been burned all over except where his shorts had been, and he screamed horribly when they sprayed his burns. They'd put him in the stiff wagon, but an army doctor felt his pulse and said, 'Hell, that man's not dead,' so they sent him here. It hurt so bad to touch him when they had to turn him for spraying that he finally persuaded the nurses to lift him by the hair on his head. But the worst thing was a Filipino girl and her three-year-old baby in the bunk next to mine. She'd lost her husband, and another child who had slipped out of her arms in the water. Kept blaming herself because her arms had got so weak he'd slid away. 'My little boy, oh, my little boy,' she kept moaning over and over.

"But meanwhile all this gloomy talk was getting me worried about the whole picture, and the next day the skipper here came in to see me—they'd sent him over on courier duty. He was looking pretty grim. When I asked him about these rumors concerning the air corps, he said it had practically been annihilated—we only had six P-40's left, and that was why everything was going to hell. The Japs had wiped out Clark and Nichols fields and also Iba, except for a few scattered planes. Also they had got seven of the navy's fourteen PBY's—clipped them off neatly when they had landed for gas. One of them had been the navy plane which hit Colin Kelly's battleship before he finally got it.

"Yet I couldn't see how they had done it, until a few days later when they began moving patients from the Manila hospital (it was the forerunner of evacuation, although we didn't guess that yet) into Corregidor. In the cot on my left was a Texas kid, a pilot from Clark Field. On the other side was an Ohio pilot from Iba. Texas was pretty sick, so the first night I shot the breeze with the Ohio boy. He said he'd been shot down the second day of the war. His squadron had been circling, looking for Jap planes which the listening devices had picked up out at sea, heading in from the direction of Formosa. They'd been up all morning, were almost out of gas, so decided to land and refuel. The first plane came in all right, but the second overshot the field. His plane was the third, and he said just as he put his wheels on the ground a load of bombs crashed down out of the clouds onto the other end of the field. Of course he poured the soup into her and took off. He tried to gain altitude and headed for Nichols Field, when suddenly a flight of Jap fighters popped out of the clouds. He turned and headed right for the center of it, but when he pressed the button only one of his six guns would work—the rest were jammed. He said don't ask him why—ask the guys who designed them or installed them or serviced them. His job was just to press the button, and he'd done that. There he was with two Zeros on his tail, filling him full of holes—they were explosive bullets, too; he had gashes all over where he'd been nicked. He said he dived into a near-by cloud and managed to shake them, but then his motor began to sputter—had been almost out of gas when the attack started, and the Jap bullets in his tanks had spilled the rest. So he headed her nose down out of the cloud, and as luck would have it spotted an emergency field. But his wing tip hit a tree and the plane cracked up, mashing in all the bones on the right side of his face. He'd spent a week in a native hospital on a bamboo bunk without the bones set, and now he could only mumble to me out of the left corner of his mouth.

"The next day Tex on the other side told me

36

his story. He was also a fighter pilot and his squadron had been at Clark Field—flying all morning. They'd come down to gas the planes, and the pilots were sitting around on the wings or in their cockpits, waiting orders to take off, when suddenly there was a big bang and the plane he was sitting in seemed to jump about forty feet in the air, and then pancaked back with its wings folded over the cockpit. The Japs had popped out of a cloud and let them have it. He crawled out unscratched, but he said for half an hour everything was in the wildest confusion—the Japs circling above, blowing those grounded planes around like popcorn in a hot skillet.

"The dope on the listening devices seemed to be, he said, that they had picked up the Japs a hundred miles at sea, followed them in all right, but then lost them when they were fifteen miles off the coast.

"But somebody decided the Japs must be heading for Baguio, and they were sitting there, all gassed up, waiting word to take off and intercept the Japs before they got to Baguio. Whereas, as a matter of fact, the Japs were perched in a cloud right over their own field, waiting to let them have it.

"He said after the bombing they'd managed to piece together out of the wreckage about ten per cent of the planes they'd originally had. A week later he'd cracked up landing on a soft spot on the field—a bomb crater that hadn't been properly filled—and here he was.

"The next time the skipper here dropped in on me, he said that was the dope he was getting—that we had only six P-40's left. Soon it got down to two; we called 'em the Phantom and the Lone Ranger.

"And I said, 'My God, what's going to happen to us?'"

"I told him I didn't know," said Bulkeley, "but that I'd been talking to the Admiral, who'd said that we couldn't possibly hope to hold the Philippine Islands, that Singapore and Hong Kong would fall too, unless help arrived—and soon. And probably the Dutch East Indies."

"Well, that floored me," said Kelly. "So I asked him how they were going to use the MTB's—wouldn't they let us go out on any offensive missions? He said he'd been trying to get the Admiral to let him go to Lingayen Gulf on a raid. Eighty Jap transports were up there landing troops, and our coastal batteries were having to fall back because of Jap air superiority—Jap fighters diving on the batteries and machine-gunning them until no one could take it.

"Then I asked the skipper how the infantry was holding. 'Not worth a damn,' he said. 'The strafing is just cutting them to ribbons. Not only that, but the Japs are landing tanks—a hell of a lot of automatic weapons which are just what we need and haven't got.' By the time he went out, I was as low as he was.

"That night Peggy, who was on night duty, got a few minutes off about one o'clock to come in and shoot the breeze with me. She'd been picking up a lot of stuff, and she said a bunch of our tank-corps boys had just been brought in. She told me what they'd been telling her, and finally said she guessed it wouldn't hurt if I went in and lay down for half an hour on an empty bunk next to them, so I could hear it myself.

"They'd walked two hundred kilometers barefoot. Four tankloads of them had been sent in to head off a Jap landing near Batangas—they were to go ahead of four columns of infantry and pave the way for retaking a little fishing village held by a small Jap force.

"The boys said their major had assured them the Japs had nothing bigger than 50-caliber machine guns—of course their armor would stop that. So they started on in, when all of a sudden—Bam! The Japs had waited until they got within good range, and then opened up with an anti-tank gun which knocked the doors off the lead tank, and then, because the road was too narrow for the rest to turn around on, they knocked the treads off all the others except one.

" 'Well, then what did you do?' I asked the kids.

" 'Fired about two hundred rounds of 50-caliber and four rounds of 37-millimeter cannon.'

" 'Which way were you shooting?'

" 'Every which way. You see, it all happened so fast we couldn't tell where the Jap fire was coming from. At the end of five minutes, three of those tanks ended up in the rice paddy—they were fourteen-ton light tanks—two of them with the

doors blown off, and in one of these, the Jap machine-gun fire had cut the legs off the lieutenant in
command. The others were riddled with holes.
Our tank was the only one that wasn't hurt.'

" 'So what did you do?'

" 'Tried to turn it around and get the hell out
of there. But the road was too narrow, and then
the tank got stuck in reverse, and ended up on its
side in the rice paddy.'

" 'What did the infantry do?'

" 'Ran like rabbits.'

" 'Didn't they have any guns?'

" 'Only rifles—not a machine gun in the crowd.
Maybe they didn't have anything else to give them,
but anyway the major said all they would find
up there was rifles, and if there were any Jap machine guns, the tanks would deal with that. So
there they were, being cut to ribbons by concealed
machine-gun fire, and nothing else to do but get
for cover.'

" 'Didn't all this—sending those tanks into a trap
without scouting ahead—seem like a damn-fool
maneuver to you?' I asked him.

" 'Well,' the kid said, 'the major and the lieu-

41

tenant had worked out the same maneuver at armored school back in the States. It had worked there; they thought it was pretty good.'

"So I asked the kid why he thought it hadn't worked this time.

" 'Maybe because the Japs were too clever in hiding their anti-tank guns and too good shots. They knocked the treads and doors off most of the tanks before they had time to do anything. And then, unlike the roads back in the States, these were narrow native roads, with rice paddies on both sides—you couldn't maneuver.'

" 'But what happened to your tank?' I asked him.

" 'We were lying on our side in that paddy, and the Japs would come over and look at us. We played possum in there all day. They tried to open our door with bayonets, but we had it locked. In the afternoon a Jap officer looked at us through the slots—all of us lying still, holding our breath, and then he said, in English, "They're all dead."

" 'But we figured it was a trick—kept right on playing possum and, sure enough, in about an hour they came back for another look. But we were lying in exactly the same positions. This time they gave a few disgusted grunts and walked off. About an hour after dark we listened carefully, and then unlocked our door. Sure enough, they'd gone, so we beat it for the road.'

" 'Tell me what became of your shoes,' I asked him. I couldn't figure how an experienced soldier would ever let himself get separated from his shoes. The kid grinned sheepishly. 'I guess that was a damn-fool trick,' he said. 'You see it had been hotter than hell in that tank, and we were all dirty and tired and sweaty, so we decided to take a bath in a creek just across the rice paddy. But we had to go through mud to get there, so, keeping our clothes on until we got to the water hole, we took off our shoes and hid them in the tall grass. But when we got back we hunted for several hours, and we couldn't find that grass clump. Finally we started on, barefooted.'

" 'But where were the Japs?'

" 'They'd gone on ahead toward Manila. The next night we were resting by the roadside. We heard a noise behind us, so we scooted low in the bushes by the side of the road, and saw more of

43

them go by on bicycles—all headed toward Manila. It seemed to be a Jap reconnaissance patrol, because behind them came trucks and guns and infantry, going by in the dark—so close we could have reached out and touched them. If we'd had a machine gun, we could have wiped out several hundred, but we only had our 45's. They kept up most of that night—one group stopped and ate chow on the road bank opposite us; we were scared stiff they'd come over and find us. It was hard for the wounded to lie quiet. Our tank driver had a rivet stuck in his throat—every time he took a drink, the water would come leaking out—and the radio operator's arm was full of shrapnel from an exploding bullet. The rest of us were okay, but our feet were getting god-damned sore.

" 'At dawn we stopped by a native village to collect some shoes, but their feet were all too small.'

" 'How'd they treat you?'

" 'Fine—gave us all the food we could eat, but you could see they didn't want us around. Afraid the Japs would find us hiding there and shoot them too. You couldn't blame the natives. So we got out, and spent the other six days of the trip sleeping in ditches or brush clumps, walking nights.'

" 'Were the wounded weak?'

" 'Sure, and so were we. The tank driver with the hole in his throat wanted to stop—said for us to leave him behind. We were afraid the Japs would get him and we couldn't spare him a gun—we had only three 45's for the six of us.'

" 'What did you do, carry him?'

" 'Hell, no. We gave him a 45, told him he'd better use it now if he wasn't coming with us. So he changed his mind, and decided to come on. He made it, too. But it took plenty of guts.'

"None of them lacked that." Here Kelly shook his head. "Sometimes training, often equipment, but never guts—and that went for the air force, too. Up to then everybody had been cussing out the god-damned air corps for letting us down. But after I talked to those pilots I knew they hadn't. They'd done the best job they could with the experience and equipment and leadership they had. Yet how slow everybody learns in a war. Nobody knows anything about a war until it begins. Just two years before, the Polish air force had been

45

blown to hell on the ground. The French caught it the following spring. In spite of that, the same thing happened to our planes at Pearl Harbor. And yet two days later, in spite of all of it, the Japs catch our air corps on Luzon with its pants down. Only that wasn't the end. Months later, on my way out through Australia, I pass a big American field, and there they are, bombers and fighters parked in orderly rows, wing tip to wing tip. 'Hell,' they told me, 'the Japs are hundreds of miles away.' Except that's where they're always supposed to be when they catch you with your pants down, and I thought to myself, Jesus Christ, won't these guys ever learn?

"But getting back to that hospital. I went back to my bunk. Peggy helped me get my arm settled, and we talked a little bit. She was a smart girl. Having been with the Regular Army, she knew real soldiers when she saw them, and you didn't have to talk long with these poor brave kids who were so green they forgot their shoes to know what the score was. Here we were, trying to hold off the Japs with less than two thousand regulars, plus these green kids who had really been sent here to polish off their training, plus thousands of Filipino boys just as brave but just as green, most of whom had never been in uniform until a few weeks before the war started. All of them up against seasoned, well-equipped fighters.

"We should have known the score then, but we didn't want to believe it. Because I was the only naval officer there, they kept riding me about the fleet.

" 'Where in hell's the navy?' they'd ask me. 'Why aren't they bringing us tanks and planes and more men? It only takes two weeks to get here from Pearl Harbor.' Of course none of them knew what had happened at Pearl Harbor.

" 'They'll be along,' I'd say. 'Any day now.'

" 'Hell,' they'd say disgustedly. 'We won't see them for six months.'

" 'Suppose we don't,' I'd say. 'This place can last six months. Wasn't it built like Malta and Gibraltar—to withstand siege?'

"Only pretty quick I began to find out how wrong I was. Corregidor had been built years ago, and then we'd agreed not to modernize if the Japs didn't modernize the Carolines. We kept the agree-

47

ment; they didn't. Anyway, ammunition and provisions were so short the Rock would be doing good to hold out three months.

"A few days after that the nurses in my ward were buzzing around—I heard some talk about a party they were giving in their quarters that evening, inviting their boy friends, who for the most part were young army officers stationed on the Rock. And I almost fell out of my cot that afternoon when Peggy, in a seemingly offhand way, asked me if I'd like to go. It was nice, of course, to be chosen, by the girl I liked best, out of 10,999 other men on that Rock, most of whom would have given an ear just to talk to a white girl. But it got me to thinking, too. I liked her, but the other girls had said there was a young medical officer she'd been dating pretty steady—and what the hell was I? A naval officer in an army hospital—here today, gone tomorrow—so I hadn't let myself get started thinking—or tried not to, anyway.

"Naturally, I said sure I wanted to go. So Peggy said she'd see if she could fix it with the doctor. And after she got through with him, he was cer-

48

tain it would do me good, if I was back in the ward by ten.

"Here in Newport maybe you wouldn't think it was much of a party. But it was a swell night, with a big moon hanging over Manila Bay—peaceful—and best of all, the girls had broken out with their civilian dresses. That doesn't sound like much, but one look at them after seeing nothing but uniforms for months was like a trip back home. Make-up too—they looked so god-damned nice you could eat them with a spoon, and Peggy had put just a touch of perfume in her hair—anyway if it wasn't that, it was something. What did we do? Well, danced to a portable—I'll bet we played 'Rose of San Antone' a dozen times—and Peggy and I figured out a way we could dance with my arm in a sling. And afterward we sat out on the grass and talked. I remember someone saying, 'You think they'll ever bomb this place?' Of course we knew eventually they would, but that night the war seemed a thousand miles away. Only somebody spoiled it all by asking Peggy when this medical officer was getting back from Bataan, and she said she thought tomorrow.

49

"Next day I was out in the courtyard getting some fresh air—I was allowed a certain number of hours per day out of my bunk—when the air-raid alarm went off, but by now we didn't pay any attention. I looked up to notice that nine Jap planes were going overhead, but what the hell, they did that all the time, and of course the anti-aircraft opened up—just a formality, because they were up out of range—when all of a sudden—Bam! the whole Rock seemed to jump, and we made a dive for the tunnel, because at last they were bombing us.

"It was quite a pasting. Half an hour later a batch of nurses came in in an ambulance—pretty well shaken up. They'd been strafed—had to leave the ambulance and run for the roadside ditches. A few minutes later the wounded began to come in—all the serious cases went into my ward. They had only two operating tables, so the litters were lined up, waiting their turn, while the nurses pitched in and took care of the minor surgery— cleaning wounds, digging for shrapnel, bandaging. There was no time for anaesthetics except a quarter of a grain of morphine, but the wounded

50

certainly had guts. They'd grab the side of their litter with clenched fists, and tell the nurses to go to it—it really wasn't hurting much.

"The raid had been going an hour when all of a sudden the lights went out, but in half a minute the girls had produced flashlights. I remember Peggy standing there holding a flashlight on a guy's naked back on the operating table while a doctor probed for some shrapnel in his kidney. You could see her face and those steady blue-green eyes of hers by the light reflected back up from this guy's back, and just then there was a terrific crunching bang—a bomb had landed right outside the tunnel entrance—and with it a sudden blast of air through the tunnel. It wasn't nice, and yet I don't think Peggy's hand even wobbled.

"Presently the lights came on, and we found one hospital-corps man had crawled under a bed. He wasn't even sheepish. 'You're damn right I was scared,' he said. 'Thought the whole place was coming down on us.' Peggy's flashlight beam on that naked back had not moved. Hell of a fine, nervy girl to have in a war. Or any other time.

"But it was getting on toward New Year's, and

bad news began to come from Manila. The Japs were closing in."

"But very few of them realized it in Manila," said Akers. "I was there with my boat on courier duty from December 13 until Manila fell. Staying with Admiral Hart until the seaplane took him out to join the Dutch East Indies fleet.

"You certainly couldn't criticize morale. The average Filipino had a childish belief in us. He was absolutely certain that the Americans would be there next week with plenty of equipment. Dead-sure that our American soldiers would throw back the Japanese. Believed all the optimistic broadcasts and rumors.

"When a raid would come, of course, they were pretty excitable. We slept aboard the boat, and when the bombs started down, we were supposed to get away from the wharf and out into the bay. Sometimes people used to stow away, to get away from the bombs.

"They never lost faith, though. Right up to the end there were big dances at the Manila Hotel, and you could watch the Filipino boys in uniform, telling their girls about their heroic exploits. **And** there were plenty of them to tell, too.

"But over at the American Army and Navy Club, they knew what the score was. They didn't feel like dancing there. Their faces were plenty long.

"Of course the higher-up Filipinos knew the truth. If you'd see one with a long face, you could be sure he was a Senator, or better.

"I had a girl there—Dolores was her first name, and by American standards she was good-looking as hell. Her father was a Spaniard from Catalonia and her mother was a mestiza. She'd been elected Miss Philippines a year or so before. Fairly tall and lithe, with big black eyes and enough of the Oriental so you'd never forget her face among the other brunettes you know.

"Her father I think was a Senator, and the family had a hell of a lot of money. His brother owned a lot of mines. They had a big colonial house in the suburbs. Usually when I was invited out she'd send a car down for me, but the first time I was coming out alone she said never mind about directions—and so it turned out. Every traffic cop I met knew just who they were and could point me on my way. So they were really big shots on the island.

"Her father knew what the score was, although Dolores didn't dream it was coming so soon. The last time I saw her, just before the Japs came in, she knew Manila had been declared an open city, but she thought that only meant there wouldn't be any more bombs. All that night the southern army had been moving through Manila, trying to get to Bataan before they were cut off, but she didn't know what the marching meant. That night her uncle, a tough old Spaniard who had mines all over the world, got pretty drunk and almost had a row with her father, the Senator.

"The uncle said the whole mess was the fault of this opposition faction of Filipino politicians hollering their silly heads off for independence—no wonder the Americans, if they were getting out in four more years, hadn't socked a lot of money into fortifications. Then he cussed the Filipino politicians out for not appropriating money for the army—they'd set MacArthur up with a big salary and a penthouse, and then hardly given him a dime to train and equip an army—it was all window-dressing.

"He said he wasn't so worried about himself because he owned plenty of property outside the islands. But he told the Senator he'd probably end up pulling a ricksha for his part in this independence foolishness, and serve him damned well right. So I could see there were a few natives who knew what the score was.

"Twelve hours before the Japs entered the town I was sent back into Manila to pick up the remnants. I had just eighty gallons of gas to go those thirty miles—finally got back with ten. A curious thing happened during those closing hours; nobody had given orders to blow up the oil reserves. Maybe some of them belonged to private companies; it would go against a businessman's grain to blow up good oil. Finally a little junior-grade naval lieutenant noticed it. He had no authority, but he gave orders he had no right to give, and presently the oil was blazing. I hear he got a Navy Cross for doing it.

"There had been quite a few pro-Jap Filipinos —not a lot in terms of percentage, but more than

you might guess. They hated the Americans because they felt inferior to us, and they weren't
quite sure we'd really give them independence in
four more years. But they weren't organized, and
they'd run around in the most childish way doing
silly things—such as flashing mirrors from the roof-
tops, when the Japs knew perfectly well where the
town was. The Filipino police caught and shot
quite a few of them."

"I was in Manila about that time," said Cox. "A
big air attack was going on, although it had already been declared an open city. For that reason
I had gone in with the guns on my boat with their
canvas covers on—for welfare reasons. Yet, open
city or not, the big air raid was on—streets deserted
except for a few people running nowhere in particular like crazy, planes crisscrossing the sky
above. The big church, about a mile from shore,
was just beginning to burn. In the harbor, boats
were burning and sinking on all sides—five- and
ten-thousand tonners. But not a single shot was
fired at the planes—which came down as low as
five hundred feet.

"I went on up into the city, and everywhere

people were kind and helpful. The Japs were right outside the town, and yet the storekeepers would give me anything we Americans needed without either money or a voucher—just sign a paper, that was all. They trusted us."

"I took my boat into the harbor just as the Japs were entering the city," said Bulkeley. "It was night, and we could see the town burning—a huge death-pall of smoke hanging above and oil six inches deep over the water. It looked like doom hanging over a great city, and it was. Made you feel bad. We stayed out there from nine o'clock at night until about three in the morning. Didn't dare go ashore, and anyway our job was to destroy harbor shipping—so what was left of it wouldn't fall into Jap hands. The little boats we'd just knock in the bottom with an ax. The big ones we'd climb aboard and set a demolition charge to. Between times we'd turn and look at the doomed city in the light of its own fires. The streets were deserted, and it was very quiet. Now and then, way off down a street, we'd see a column of Jap infantry or some cyclists go by. There was still some firing from the direction of Nichols Field.

57

The big American Army and Navy Club was dark and deserted on the water front, but presently lights began to come on—the Japs were taking over. They made it their headquarters. Watching those lights come on made you plenty sore."

"I had to leave all my spare uniforms in my locker there, damn them," said Akers. "I hope none of them fit."

"Watching them take over made you feel pretty sick," said Bulkeley. "We finished up and started home, to get back before dawn, now and then looking back at the fires over the water. Every time it made us sore."

"It was a tough New Year's Eve for me, too," said Kelly, "because we knew more or less what was going on. Then there was another reason. Some of the army officers were throwing a little New Year's party with the nurses that night, and since this medical officer Peggy had been going with was just back from Bataan, of course I knew where she'd be.

"Along in the evening after sunset I walked out to the mouth of the tunnel and sat down, to watch the twilight of the old year die away. It had been a tough year, but the one ahead looked worse. And here was I, useless for the war, in an army hospital. From away off I could hear them playing the portable at the officers' party, and I remembered how cute Peggy had looked in her civilian dress when she danced, and that didn't help any. Pretty soon one of the other nurses I knew, Charlotte, came out and sat down near me. She wasn't at the party because she had to go on duty soon, but that didn't matter, because her boy friend had just been wounded three days before, and she was worried sick about him. She told me, and began to cry while she was telling it, that they were planning to load him on a hospital ship which was due to sail for Australia soon. She said she wouldn't mind being left behind and being captured by the Japanese—it wasn't that, it was because she was afraid his ship would be torpedoed—never get through.

"Just then I noticed someone sitting down on the other side of me—I turned and, by George, it was Peggy. Not in uniform, either. She was wearing that cute cool-looking cotton-print civilian dress.

59

"I couldn't figure it. 'Didn't you like the party?' I asked. 'Wasn't it any good?'

" 'I don't know,' she said. 'I didn't go to the party.'

" 'Weren't you asked?'

" 'Yes,' she said. 'I was asked. But it was New Year's, you see, and I thought it might be nice here.'

"Not very many nice things happen to you during a war, but this was about the nicest that ever happened to me then, or any other time. It made me feel so good that between the two of us, we managed to get Charlotte cheered up. She had to go back on duty presently, and she managed to sneak us out a couple of fairly cold bottles of Pabst beer, to celebrate on. But Peggy had been preparing. The island was on two meals a day, but she'd managed to hold back a couple of apples and a whole box of marshmallows. That was our New Year's Eve supper, and I'll bet that yours, wherever you had it, couldn't have tasted any better.

"Running any kind of romance, no matter how mild, was a real problem on Corregidor. About the best place to sit was right where we were, at the tunnel's mouth. But the road ran right in front of it, and every five minutes an army truck would barge tactlessly around the curve, shining its dimmed-down headlights right on you. Then for another three minutes you were choking with dust. If you got tired of this and tried to go for a walk, you'd hardly get started when you would realize that eleven thousand men were trying to sleep all over that little island, and if you went far, you would step on most of them in the dark, and not many of them would thank you for it. There wasn't an unoccupied square foot anywhere.

"We proved that later on when the doctor prescribed walks for me—to build back my strength, because I'd lost thirty pounds—and Peggy was assigned to go along. The troops swarmed on that island—every pond was crowded with them bathing, and I would always have to go ahead to take a look over hilltops and be sure Peggy wouldn't surprise them.

"Meanwhile Bulkeley was reporting to the Admiral daily and was formulating a plan—which he would talk over with me, as I was his second officer —for what we would do when our gas ran out. We had damned little left, and the army couldn't spare us any.

"Our first plan was, when we got down to our minimum, to get out to Australia. The navy patrol bombers had planted caches of gasoline among the islands like steppingstones, and the Admiral gave us their location. But the first steppingstone was Singapore, and the Japs were working their way down the peninsula, closer and closer to it. Could we get there first? Of course we wouldn't leave the Philippines until all of our torpedoes were gone and we had just enough gas left to make the final run. But then, as you know, Singapore fell and also the southern islands—Celebes and Zamboanga. The route with the cached gas was closed— that plan was out.

"So then we said, who wanted to go to Australia anyway? Our job was to defend Manila Bay— wasn't that our part in the war plan? Yet even then it kept coming up: suppose the worst came to the worst and Luzon folded up—the whole archipelago—even Java—what then?

"Then Bulkeley here hit on a real plan. When our gas was down to just what we could carry on

our decks, instead of waiting around to get captured by the Japs, we'd take our boats to China to
continue the war. At first glance you'd say that
was crazy—the Japanese holding most of the Chinese coast—but not the way the skipper had it
thought out. He knew China from the years he'd
spent out there on a gunboat while I was there on
a destroyer.

"The Japs were closing in on Hong Kong—that
was fine for us! We'd make our dash—shoot our
last few remaining fish at their gathered transports
just where they least expected an attack, and then
head north toward the region of Swatow.

"Of course the Japs held that coast too, but
Bulkeley had worked out an answer, all in the ut-
most secrecy. He'd gotten in touch with Colonel
Wong, the Chinese military observer. Wong had
cabled Chungking to investigate the vicinity.
Chungking cabled back that it could be done.

"They said the Japs held the Swatow region
thinly—at no point did they go more than ten
miles inland. So, at an agreed time, and at an
agreed rendezvous on the coast, Chungking would

send a raiding party down to fight its way to the beach and meet us.

"There we would burn our boats—now useless with all torpedoes expended against Jap targets. The Chinese couldn't hold that point long—but long enough to hustle us through that ten-mile Jap-held strip onto free Chinese soil. There trucks would take us to the nearest airfield, we would fly to Chungking, and from there a four-motored American ferry-command plane would bring us back to the States.

"Where was the flaw? We couldn't see one, unless somehow it leaked out. Besides myself, only four living people knew. They were DeLong of our squadron, Captain Ray, chief of staff, Colonel Wong, and of course the skipper here, who had worked out every detail.

"But before we left we knew there would be plenty of action ahead for us here, and I told Bulkeley I was crazy to get out of this hospital, and asked for his help. If they'd let me get back to duty, I'd agree to anything—promise to soak my hand for so many hours a day—anything they said, just to get back even on a semiduty status.

"So we staged it for the next morning, when the ward doctor would be dressing my hand at about the same time the head surgeon made his rounds. We tackled him. I made my talk, and he seemed to waver. 'Tell this bird you need me,' I said to the skipper. 'We really do,' said Bulkeley, but just then Peggy overheard and queered the whole thing. 'Certainly not!' she said. 'You can't let him go back to duty with his hand wide-open!' That swung him back. 'Duty!' he growled. 'Who said anything about duty? Two weeks of it and you'd lose your whole arm.'

"I tried to argue—point out that if the MTB's went out on a mission, I could hold on with one arm as well as two, but Peggy had done it, and now he wouldn't listen.

" 'One of these days you're going to find an empty bunk,' I said. I was gloomy all that next week, but Peggy said I was a fool. That there were plenty of well, fit men to do my job. And that if I hadn't been so damned stubborn in the first place, and had got that hand treated in time, I'd never have come to the hospital, and never met her, and she would never have been able to break up my plan to get out, so it was all my fault!

"She always had that cute way of seeming to storm at you and dress you down, so that you ended up by grinning and couldn't stay mad at anything long.

"So it went along for another week, she leading me out for walks every day to get some of those thirty pounds back, and then one day we returned to find that Bulkeley had been by looking for me—said he was going out on a raid that night, up to Subic Bay looking for a Jap cruiser, that he'd waited hoping to take me, but finally had to leave.

"It set me almost crazy. If I hadn't been out on that god-damned health tour with a pretty girl, I wouldn't have missed the raid! So here I was while my gang was up there tangling with a cruiser, maybe getting killed, because the Japs had Subic Bay so thick with guns that it was almost suicide to go in.

"All that night there was no news. I was up at 5:30—'Any dope from the torpedo boats?'—still nothing. But at seven they said, yes, Bulkeley had come back, managed to sink a cruiser and get away, but the other boat was missing—probably lost."

"It was a job we did for the army," explained Bulkeley. "A couple of Jap ships, one of them an Imperial Navy auxiliary cruiser with 6-inch guns had been shelling out 155-millimeter emplacements on Bataan—blasting them with heavy stuff. The major in charge had been wondering how to get rid of them and had phoned Admiral Rockwell, who gave us permission to tackle the job. We knew they were based in Subic Bay, probably in Port Binanga. Subic is on the west coast of Luzon, just north of Bataan. I decided to send two boats—the 31 boat, which was Lieutenant DeLong's, and the 34 boat, which was Kelly's, now commanded by Ensign Chandler. I went along in it for the hell of it.

"We tested everything—tuned the motors, greased torpedoes, and got under way at nine o'clock, chugging north along the west coast of Bataan. It was very rough. We throttled down to thirty knots, and even then we were shipping water, but we got off the entrance to Subic Bay about half an hour after midnight. Here, according to plan, the two boats separated. DeLong in the 31 boat was to sweep one side of Subic Bay and I the other. We were to meet at Port Binanga, at the end. If something happened and we didn't meet there, then we were to rendezvous at dawn just outside the mine fields of Corregidor.

"So we separated, expecting to meet at dawn. It was the last I ever saw of the 31 boat. But here's what happened to our 34 boat in Subic. First, remember it was darker than hell, and the shore line was loaded with Jap field guns. None of us had ventured in there since the Japs took over. We had got in just a little way when a Jap searchlight spotted us and blinked out a dot-dash challenge, asking who we were. Since we didn't know the Jap code reply, naturally we didn't answer, but changed course, veering away. But the Japs were getting suspicious by now, and from over by Ilinin Point a single field piece opened up. None of it fell near us—maybe they were shooting at DeLong in the 31 boat.

"When we were about abeam of Sueste light another light came on to challenge us—this time from a ship, maybe that cruiser. We changed course to

68

go over and have a look, but she was small fry—
not worth a torpedo—the hell with her—we were
headed for Binanga and the cruiser

"By this time the Japs over on Grande Island
realized something funny was going on—their light
challenged us, but of course we didn't answer.
Then they broke out some 50-caliber machine-gun
fire at us from Ilinin Point. We could see the
tracers feeling for us, and then the fun started—big
3-inch shore batteries rumbling all over the bay
and lights feeling for us. We could hear the shells
whistle over our heads in the dark, and could have
done without some of them. But the lights and
flashes from the shore batteries were a real help,
for they enabled us to pick out the shore line, so,
in spite of the fact that it was blacker than hell,
we knew where we were.

"By one o'clock we were off the north entrance
to Port Binanga, where we were to meet DeLong
in the 31 boat and go in together for the attack,
and when he didn't show up, I began to be afraid
something might have happened, yet I couldn't be
sure.

"But there was nothing to do but go on in alone.

69

To make the sneak, we cut the speed down to eight knots, skirted Chiquita Island, rounded Binanga Point, and entered the little bay on two engines at idling speed. Everything was quiet, no firing down here, and then we saw her ahead in the dark not five hundred yards away. Creeping up on her, we had just readied two torpedoes when a searchlight came on and in dot-dash code she asked us who we were.

"We answered, all right—with two torpedoes—but they had hardly been fired when I gave our boat hard rudder and started away. It isn't safe for an MTB to stay near a cruiser. One torpedo hit home with a hell of a thud—we heard it over our shoulders. Looking back, we saw the red fire rising, and presently two more explosions which might have been her magazines.

"But we had no time for staring, for we were into plenty trouble. One of those torpedoes had failed to clear its tube and was stuck there, just at the entrance, and was making what we call a 'hot run,' its propellers buzzing like hell, compressed air hissing so you couldn't hear yourself think. But worst of all, a torpedo is adjusted so that it won't

70

fire until its propeller has made a certain number
of revolutions—I shouldn't give it exactly, but let's
say it is three hundred. After that, the torpedo is
cocked like a rifle, and an eight-pound blow on its
nose would set it off—blowing us all to glory.

"So what to do? Somehow that torpedo propeller had to be stopped and stopped quick, or else
a good hard wave slap on the torpedo's nose would
blow us all to splinters. And at this point our torpedoman, Martino, used his head fast. He ran to
the head and swiped a handful of toilet paper. He
jumped astride that wobbling, hissing torpedo like
it was a horse, and, with the toilet paper, jammed
the vanes of the propeller, stopping it.

"We'd stopped for all this, but we couldn't af-
ford to wait long. The cruiser's fire was lighting up
the bay behind us. Ahead, all over Subic, hell was
breaking loose. So we started up, gave her everything we had to get through that fire.

"With four motors roaring, and us skipping
around in that rough water with everything wide-
open, I guess we made considerable commotion.
Anyway the Japanese radio in Tokyo, reporting
the attack next day, said the Americans had a new

secret weapon—a monster that roared, flapped its
wings, and fired torpedoes in all directions. It was
only us, of course, but we felt flattered. We got
the hell out of there, and that was all there was
to it."

"Well," said Kelly, "MacArthur wouldn't quite
agree. He gave you the D.S.C. for what you'd
done."

"But DeLong has the real story," insisted Bulkeley. "I pulled up outside the mine field off Corregidor to wait for him. Neither of us could go in until
it got light, because otherwise the army on shore,
hearing us in the dark out there, would think it
was Japs and set off the mine field. But when the
sky got light and I saw my boat was alone, I realized DeLong was in trouble. And since he's now
a prisoner of the Japanese—if he's alive—we'd better tell his story for him.

"After we parted company at the entrance to
Subic Bay, he started around its northern rim as
we'd planned. But just before midnight he developed engine trouble—the saboteur's wax had
clogged his strainers. He cleaned them and had just
got under way when more trouble developed—the

cooling system went haywire. They stopped, and were drifting as they repaired it when there was an ominous grinding sound under the boat—they were aground on a reef in Subic Bay. At any minute a wandering Jap searchlight might pick them up and artillery fire would blow them to bits.

"They rocked the boat, and finally started the engines to get themselves unstuck. But the noise now attracted the Japs, and a 3-inch gun on Ilinin Point opened up on them—splashes coming nearer and nearer. They worked frantically, finally burned out all reverse gears so that the engines were useless. DeLong gave orders to abandon ship. They wrapped mattresses in a tarpaulin to make a raft, and all got aboard but DeLong, who stayed to chop holes in the gas tanks and blow a hole in the boat's bottom with a hand grenade before he jumped. That was the end of the 31. Then he couldn't find the raft in the darkness, and being afraid to call out, swam to the beach.

"The raft had shoved off with all twelve aboard at three o'clock.

"He waited on the sands until dawn. Then, in the gray half-light, he picked up the tracks of nine men. He followed these until they led into a clump of bushes, where he found most of his crew. They explained they had stayed with the raft until dawn was about to break. Fearing sunrise would expose them to the Japanese, they had decided to risk a swim to the beach, where they could hide. But Ensign Plant and two men, who couldn't swim very well, decided to stay. What became of them the nine didn't know, and no one knows for sure to this day.

"But the first thing DeLong did was to post lookouts, and all day they stayed in that clump, with an eye on the Jap observation planes which flew over them in relays, watching a hot little skirmish between the Americans and the Japanese on the far shore of the bay. At one point the Japs were falling back, and there seemed to be a chance that they could make a run for it in daylight, rejoining the American lines. But never was it quite possible, and in the meantime they had spotted a couple of bancas, native boats, farther down the beach.

"Two men who were sent out to investigate, crawling on their bellies through the grass, returned to report the bancas were in fair condition. So when the sun had set they crawled to them and started getting them in shape. For rowing they had two paddles, a couple of spades, and a board. They had to work fast and quietly, for the Japs were all around them—just as they were launching the bancas they heard Japanese voices not two hundred yards away.

"But a heavy wind came up, and at nine o'clock at night, both boats capsized. They righted them, but the shovels and the board were lost, and they now had only one paddle for each banca. Yet with these they continued to fight the head wind until three in the morning, when they were so exhausted that they decided to try the shore. So DeLong landed on what he hoped was Napo Point. They picked their way through the barbed-wire entanglement on the beach, and then found themselves up against a steep cliff.

"They kept very quiet until dawn, not knowing whether daylight would find them surrounded by Americans or Japanese. But when it became light, the first thing they saw was a Filipino sentry.

" 'Hey, Joe—got a cigarette and a match?' they

75

called out. And an hour later they were telling their story to Captain Cockburn, in the Ninety-second American Infantry's field headquarters tent. The nine were back with us at Sisiman Cove the next evening."

"But we'd never really expected to see them again," said Kelly. "And when I heard only one boat had come back from Subic Bay, I got hold of my doctor.

" 'Now you've *got* to let me go!' I said. 'Here we've lost the third officer of the squadron. There's a war on, and I've spent all the time I intend to nursing a sore finger.'

"That afternoon Bulkeley came over to tell me the story of the engagement. When he was through, 'Kelly,' he said, 'we need you.'

" 'Let's get ahold of that doctor,' I said, 'and you tell him that.' This time it worked. The hole in my finger was still almost three inches long and about an inch wide, with some of the tendon exposed (but in a month it was healed, except that I can't move my finger joints). I had to promise them faithfully I would show up every other day

76

for treatment, but the point of it was I got out of that place.

"Two days later I took the 34 boat out on my first patrol from Corregidor up along Bataan toward Subic Bay—Bulkeley, who as squadron commander rode all boats on patrol, of course was with me. It was a calm night—and chilly. Sweaters were comfortable over our khakis, although in the daytime we wore only shorts or trunks. The rest of the men were burned black as natives, but I was still pale from the hospital.

"Everything was going well, in fact it was monotonous. But when we were about twenty-five miles up the coast, hell suddenly started popping. Our own batteries were shooting at us. Bulkeley explained to me that was the main excitement these days—to keep from being sunk by your own side— and calmly altered course to get out of their range, which we could tell by the light of their tracer bullets.

" 'Half the time those dumb dastards don't know friend from foe,' he explained.

"Five minutes later we saw a dim light, low in the water, and headed toward it. Was it a Jap land-

77

ing barge, trying to get ashore behind General Wainwright's lines? Then it occurred to us that it might be Ensign Plant and the two other men of DeLong's boat who had disappeared in Subic Bay. They might have stolen a boat and now be headed home—we couldn't take chances. So without firing we drew nearer, watching the light.

"Presently it began to blink—dots and dashes, all right, but no message that we could read. Bulkeley ordered general quarters as a precaution, and the men were crouching behind their machine guns. It was about twenty-five yards away now—a queer-shaped boat, low in the water—and suddenly its light went out.

"Bulkeley stood up with the megaphone. 'Boat ahoy!' he called. He got a quick answer. Br-r-r-r-r! They opened on him with machine guns. It looked like a fire hose of tracer bullets headed for our cockpit, and now they speeded up, trying to head for shore. But we were pouring the fire back at them. Our four 50-calibers were rattling away, Bulkeley had picked up an automatic rifle and was pumping it into them, and even the men down in the engine room, hearing the row, had grabbed their rifles and come up to fire over the sides.

"Now we could see it was a Jap landing barge, packed with men. It had armor on the bow and the stern, and kept twisting and turning, trying to keep those thick steel plates pointed toward us. Of course our maneuver was to come in from the side, and let them have it where they couldn't take it, as we circled them.

"All this had been going on for about thirty seconds when I heard a cry of pain from behind. It was Ensign Chandler. 'I've been hit,' he said. A Jap bullet had gone through both of his ankles. We pulled him out of the cockpit and laid him down on the canopy, meanwhile circling the Japs and pouring the steel down into their vulnerable sides. We could soon see we were getting them. The barge sank lower and lower in the water and presently gurgled under, while we pulled off to lick our own wounds, give first aid to Chandler, and locate any other boats in the vicinity. Surely the Japs wouldn't attempt a landing with a single barge. All we got, though, was more fire from our own shore guns—a swarm of tracers and then

3-inchers began whistling over—one of them landing two hundred yards away. But we didn't mind.
The army seemed to enjoy it, and it wasn't hurting us.

"We fooled around until almost dawn and were
headed for home—we couldn't have got Chandler
through the mine fields to the hospital until sunrise
anyway, when Bulkeley happened to glance back.

"Through the half-light he could see, bobbing
in the swell, another low-lying flat craft. Should
we go back? You're god-damned right we should,
the men said—to get even for Chandler by sinking
some more of them.

"As we got closer, sure enough, it was another
landing boat, this time apparently leaving the coast
of Bataan, and we opened up on her with everything we had from four hundred yards away.

"But their return fire was curiously light and
spasmodic. So we closed to about ten yards. Their
fire had stopped, but their boat wouldn't. Our bullets would hit its armor and engines—you could
see the tracers bounce off and ricochet one hundred feet into the air, but still it kept going. Suddenly a tracer hit its fuel tanks—up they went in

a blaze, the motor stopped, and now the boat was only drifting. But even as we pulled alongside, those Japs, nervy devils, gave her hard rudder and tried to ram us. So Bulkeley tossed in a couple of hand grenades from about twenty feet away, and that took the fight out of them. We went alongside, and Bulkeley jumped aboard her—into about a foot of water, blood, and oil, for she was sinking fast. We'd been firing almost diagonally down through her sides and bottom.

"She was empty except for three Japs—must have discharged her landing party and been headed home. One was dead, two were wounded, and one of these two was a Jap officer.

"Bulkeley had his 45 in his hand when he jumped aboard, and immediately this Jap officer went to his knees and began to call, 'Me surrender! —Me surrender!' "

"He was talking fast," said Bulkeley a little grimly, "and he had his hands stuck up very high and stiff, and that ought to stop the myth about how Japs are too noble ever to surrender. I put a line around his shoulders and we hoisted him aboard the 34 boat.

"Then I began rummaging around in that sludge for papers, brief cases, and knapsacks. I collected, among other things, the muster list of the landing party and their operations plan, before the boat sank beneath me—Kelly pulled me into his boat as the barge sank.

"One of our men was standing guard over the Jap captain with a 45, and the captain was kneeling with his eyes closed, waiting for what he was sure would be the final shot. He would hardly believe it wasn't coming even when I wiped the oil out of his eyes and looked at his head wound. When he found we weren't going to shoot him, he got a little surly. The soldier asked for a cigarette, but when I offered the Jap captain one, he shook his head. Pretended he didn't speak English, but when they got him back to base, Intelligence found he spoke plenty, but wouldn't tell them anything."

"A queer thing had happened to us," said Kelly. "We couldn't be mad any more. Ten minutes before we'd all been pumping steel, hating every Jap in the world. Now we were sorry for these two, they were so abject, sitting there on the deck—little half-pint guys—the youngest boy in our crew looked like a full-grown man beside them. Our crew all came up to take a look. People had been scared of these guys? It seemed impossible! Any man could handle two of them in a fight. There they were, avoiding our eyes, and yet we had to hand it to them—they'd put up a damned good fight. And our crew were very much impressed by how much a few men can do if they're willing to die. The little private who sat there puffing the cigarette had five holes in him.

"Quite a few officers were waiting for us on the dock; they'd watched our fight from an observation post on Bataan but couldn't make out from the tracers what was going on or how it came out.

"We had quite a time loading Chandler and the Japs into the ambulance, because the forecastle was slippery with blood. It soaked into the sneakers we were wearing until we could hardly stand up, and by the time the Japs were loaded, it was all over our hands and pants.

"The ambulance doctor, glancing at them, said he thought the Jap officer would pull through, but that there wasn't much chance for the little private puffing the cigarette. Matter of fact, he died on the way to the field hospital at Little Baguio."

"You never know when you're going to run into something," said Bulkeley. "A couple of nights later, I was riding the 41 boat on routine patrol off the west coast of Bataan. When we began to get near to Biniptican Point, the entrance to Subic, we cut it down to one engine, to make the least possible noise. Just before ten o'clock, I spotted a Jap ship which seemed to be lying to, near shore. We called general quarters and began sneaking up on her—still using only one engine until we got within about twenty-five hundred yards. Then we gave everything the gun and roared in—but almost into a trap. Because the Japs had prepared a little welcome for us, and this ship was seemingly the bait to a trap—they had floating entanglements and wires in the water which might foul our propellers and leave us a dead target for their batteries. We saw them just in time, and now we saw they were trying to unbait the trap—because that big ship was showing a wake, trying to get under way.

"At a thousand yards we fired our first torpedo, and it had hardly hit the water before the Jap ship

84

opened up on us with a pom-pom. They'd been playing possum, waiting for us. But what the hell— we wanted to be sure we'd stolen the bait from that trap, so we went right on in, ahead of our own torpedo, and let her have another at four hundred yards. Then I gave hard rudder and as we turned abeam of her, we sprayed her decks with the 50's, and every man on board picked up a rifle and began pumping at her—just for the hell of it—and the Japs were dishing it right back, but not for many seconds. Because all of a sudden—Bam! It was our first torpedo striking home, and pieces of wreckage fell in the water all around us. The explosion gave us our first clear look at her. She was—or had been until then—a modern, streamlined 6,000-ton auxiliary aircraft carrier. Pretty expensive bait for any trap.

"But the Japs weren't through with us. A battery of about half a dozen 3-inch guns opened up on us from the shore—by the flashes we could see they were pumping it to us as fast as they could load, and they certainly took our minds off our other troubles. So with big splashes all around us, we executed that naval maneuver technically known as getting the hell out of there, swerving, weaving, avoiding those damned wire nets, and trying to figure out where the Japs would place their next artillery shots, to make sure we wouldn't be under them—giving her every ounce of gas we could stuff into those six thousand horses, until we were out of range. I think the Japs were getting tired of us MTB's, and risked exposing that ship to rid themselves of a nuisance."

"I was staying that night with Chandler at Corregidor hospital," said Kelly, "and we knew you'd had good hunting when we saw you come chugging up to the dock next morning with that broom tied to your masthead and your forward torpedo tubes empty. After that there was a little lull. I was supposed to report to the doctor every other day to have my finger dressed, and I'd go late in the afternoon and have a date with Peggy. Sometimes we'd walk down to the navy communications center at Monkey Point to pick up the radio news and gossip—often we'd just sit on the sea wall and watch the moon on the water. Sometimes wondering what would become of us. Often it would be a foursome, or we would sit out there with Stevens,

the nurse, whose boy friend was an artillery captain over on Bataan. She'd always watch the gun
flashes, which were getting closer now as the Japs
were pushing our boys farther and farther down
the peninsula. Stevens would always worry—for
fear every flash was a Jap field piece firing at her
captain. But we'd tell her we knew by the color
that it was her captain firing at the Japs.

"Early in February they started sending submarines up from Australia, and our boats would
always meet them outside the mine fields and bring
them in—Bulkeley getting aboard to ride as pilot.
The subs had news. They said America was building a big Australian base—that supplies were rolling
down there. The submarine *Trout* would bring
in ammunition for the army's 3-inch guns on
Bataan and take out gold which had been brought
over to Corregidor from Manila before it fell. The
unloading, of course, would all be at night, and
then Bulkeley would take them out and show them
deep water, where they could submerge and hide
from Jap bombers during the day. Quezon went
out on one submarine to Cebu, and a week later
High Commissioner Sayre left on a submarine. It

seemed like a good many prominent people were leaving Corregidor. And the army had been pushed back to what we knew were its last and strongest defense positions on Bataan. None of it looked too good.

"Of our original six boats, two had already been lost, DeLong's over in Subic Bay, and the 33 boat while I was in the hospital—she'd been going full speed ahead investigating what looked at night like the feather of a Japanese submarine's periscope, only it turned out to be a wave breaking over a little submerged and uncharted coral reef."

"We came close to losing the 32 boat about that time," said Bulkeley. "DeLong and I were riding her the night of February 8, patrolling up the west coast of Bataan as usual. A little before nine o'clock we saw gun blasts on up ahead of us in the neighborhood of Bagac Bay, so we put on what speed we could to find out who was shooting at what. Incidentally, the speed wasn't much. Because the 32 boat had had an explosion while they were cleaning that saboteur's wax out of her strainers and tanks, so that now she was held together with braces and wires, and running on only two engines. But pretty soon we sighted a ship dead-ahead about three miles away. I was maneuvering to put her in the path of the moonlight on the water so I could make out what she was. But now she seemed to put on speed, heading up in the direction of Subic Bay—maybe, if she had seen us, to get under the protection of the Jap shore batteries there.

"Why had she been firing near Bagac Bay? We learned that later. She was a 7,000-ton Jap cruiser covering a Jap landing party with her guns. We didn't know we'd broken up this party at the time. Following her, we seemed to be gaining because she had apparently slowed down, maybe thinking she had lost us. We were closing on her fast now, when suddenly a huge big searchlight came on, holding us directly in its beam, and a few seconds later two 6-inch shells came screaming over, landing just ahead of us with a terrific explosion and waterspout. Her searchlight was blinding us and we could only head directly into it, firing the starboard torpedo at that light at about four thousand yards' range. There was another flash of 6-inch guns from the cruiser, and this salvo dropped much closer to us—hardly two hundred yards ahead. A third two-gun salvo landed just astern of us, and then we let her have the port torpedo, figuring the range at a little over three thousand yards.

"Now we were empty, and the problem was to dodge that blinding searchlight. Before we veered off to the east, we tried to douse it with a spray of 50-caliber bullets, but they did no good. We could hardly see where our tracers went for the glare. We could see now she was chasing us, firing salvoes in pairs from her four 6-inch guns, when suddenly there was a dull boom, and we could see debris and wreckage sailing up through that searchlight's beam. There was a pause in her firing—no doubt about it, one of our torpedoes had struck home, probably the second one. We knew she was crippled because she had slowed down—that light which was trying to hold us in its glare was getting farther and farther away, and about 10:30 we lost it by making a hard turn to the right. Presently it went out. It came on again once or twice on the horizon, feeling for us over the waves, but never found us.

"The next day the army told us we'd broken up a 7,000-ton cruiser's landing party on Bataan near the village of Moron, which was then in no-man's land, and said their planes reported the Japs had had to beach her seventy-five miles up the coast. Still later the planes reported the Japs were breaking her up for scrap. But we brought the 32 boat back safe to the base at Sisiman Cove. Our headquarters there was a reformed goat slaughter-house, about one hundred feet long and thirty feet wide, with a concrete floor. We'd scrubbed it out with creosote. It still smelled some, but was habitable. We'd also acquired a tender—an old harbor tug called the *Trabajador*—and put her in charge of DeLong, who'd lost his ship."

"Then we all sat around envying him," said Kelly, "because here he was, living like an admiral —a cabin, a wardroom, a real galley (not just a hot plate, which was all we had on the MTB's), and even a mess boy who could bake pies. It was big-ship life, and Bulkeley and I used to find some excuse to go every night and eat his dessert and drink coffee. DeLong liked it so much he later de-

91

cided to stay on Bataan rather than leave with the rest of us.

"Our plan for making a run for China when our gas was almost gone still stood, and Bulkeley had got hold of some landing-force gear which we knew might be useful on the Chinese coast if we missed connections with our Chungking friends and had to fight our way through the Japs. So we began drilling our men in landing-force procedure.

"This got them very curious. They knew our gas was running out, and we had almost no more torpedoes except the ones which were in the boats. So we told them we were thinking of going south to join the Moros if Bataan fell, and it satisfied them for a while. We let only two other persons in on the secret—Clark Lee and Nat Floyd, newspaper correspondents who had been authorized by the Admiral to make the trip with us.

"The food situation was getting tough. Our breakfast was always hot cakes made without eggs —just flour, water, and baking powder—and the syrup was sugar and water. We hadn't seen butter since the war started. Then for dinner, it was always canned salmon and rice, and you don't know how tired you can get of canned salmon until you eat it regularly for a few months. We welcomed any change."

"On our boat we got so tired of salmon we ate a tomcat," said Bulkeley. "It had been bothering us at night, and one of the men plugged it with a 45. We boiled it to get all the good out of it, and it wasn't bad. All dark meat—reminded you a little of duck. Of course we didn't have to eat it—if you didn't like tomcat, there was always plenty of canned salmon."

"The one high spot in our diet was the *Canopus*," said Kelly. "She was an old sub tender, so slow she'd been abandoned, but she had a fine machine shop. She was tied up at the dock and already had been hit twice by bombs, so they worked her at night and abandoned her by day. But among her stores were barrels and barrels of ice-cream mix and a freezer. And her skipper would let anyone in the navy who came aboard eat all the ice cream he wanted as long as those barrels lasted—they held out until the week we left. So the skipper here, who is very fond of ice cream, used to go over every night and fill up.

"But what we wanted most of all was fresh meat and vegetables, and along about the second week in February the first blockade-runner arrived. We piloted her in at night—rendezvous twenty-five miles out—and as daylight came, our mouths watered as we saw her cargo, strings of bananas piled high on her decks, and below, fresh meat and fruit for Corregidor. That afternoon I went over to see Peggy, and they were all busy slicing steaks and candling eggs. By yelling, screaming, and haggling, I got enough fresh meat to serve our crews two meals that week. She was a welcome little ship, that blockade-runner—made two more trips before the Japs sank her.

"But because of Peggy, my diet was a little better than the others. Since she was on Corregidor, she was entitled, under their rationing system, to buy one item per day from the canteen—a package of gum, a candy bar maybe, from the little supply they had left.

"But Peggy pretended she never cared for them, and every time I came to see her, she'd slip me a pocketful. She bought and saved them every day

—just something to nibble while I was out on patrol, she explained.

"I began to feel funny about that break-through to China we were planning. Of course the Admiral had ordered it, and of course it was the way we could be most useful. But here were all these brave people on Bataan and the Rock, Peggy among them, realizing more clearly every day that they would never get out. Doomed, but bracing themselves to look fate in the face as it drew nearer, knowing that they were expendable like ammunition, and that it was part of the war plan that they should sell themselves as dearly as possible before they were killed or captured by the Japs. But a handful of us secretly knew that we, and only we among these many brave thousands, would see home again, and soon.

"And the more I liked Peggy—she was a swell kid—the guiltier I felt. Furthermore, I knew if we ever left, it would have to be soon. Gas was getting dangerously low—barely enough to make the run for China. And so was our torpedo supply. We would have to leave with every tube full if we were to throw effective weight against Jap

95

shipping on the China coast, and in addition to what we would need for this, we had only a few torpedoes left, enough for one good fight—and that was to come sooner than we knew."

"I'll never forget that night," said Cox, "because I had a curious assignment in the afternoon. It seems our artillery on Bataan was being bothered by long-range Jap guns which were being installed on the other shore—the Batangas side. The artillery major had appealed to Bulkeley for help. So my assignment was to take the major aboard about five in the afternoon, and ride along the Batangas shore with him, tempting the Japs. When they opened fire at us, the major would make careful note of their position.

"I hope the major got what he wanted. I know before it was over I had all I wanted of being a voluntary target for the Japanese, and my men were looking around for some targets of their own. Just then we were passing a beach, and there was a whole company of Jap infantry, no hats, stripped down to their waists, wearing white underdrawers. We thought at first they were natives, and then noticed every man had on glasses, which always gives them away. Instead of running, curiosity got the better of them—they crowded down to the water, pointing at us, and then they began to laugh and jeer, showing their crooked monkey teeth. Our boys had had about enough of it, so they broke it up by spraying them with a battery of 50-calibers, and considering what we'd been through, it felt good seeing them spinning around, or kneeling and then slumping as the bullets hit. We learned later from spies that we'd killed eight and wounded fourteen.

"We always knew just what was going on on the mainland. There was, for instance, a bamboo American—some man who'd married a Filipino wife and gone native—who managed a big pineapple plantation; he organized it into quite a system. He had a pass from the Japanese to bring vegetables into Manila. I think it was because he had a Swedish passport, although he'd lived in the States or the islands almost all his life and spoke without an accent. For three dollars he'd deliver a message from Corregidor to anyone in Manila. And for one hundred dollars he would bring anyone out of Manila and deliver him to Corregidor

—if he didn't mind being buried under pineapples in his wagon for a while. We got our report on the casualties from him."

"When we went out that night," said Bulkeley, "we didn't dream we were to take our final crack at the Japs off Bataan. I took two boats—Kelly in the 34, riding myself with Akers in the 35—to see if we couldn't bag one of the Jap destroyers which the army could see in Subic Bay. They'd been driven pretty far back, but from the highest ridge of the Bataan mountains they could still look down into Subic with their 20-power binoculars.

"But the Admiral had said we weren't to go into the bay. We must coax them outside. The Japs had the bay's rim lined with guns, and it would be suicide. We got outside of Subic about eleven o'clock. All according to plan, Kelly hid his 34 boat in a cove just outside the bay, while I went into the entrance and raised a little hell—fired my machine guns so they could see the tracers, hoping a Jap destroyer would follow me out, whereupon Kelly was to come out of the cove and lam a couple of torpedoes into their engine room. It didn't work. The Japs had had all they wanted of us. But just as I was about to leave, I saw from the entrance the outline of a big ship—tied to Olongapo dock."

"She was a big one," said Akers, "maybe 10,000 tons. A tanker, we learned the next day. So we turned back, sneaked toward her—there was no fire on us yet—and cut loose two torpedoes. By the time they exploded, we had cleared the mouth of the bay. But from the mountains of Bataan the army watched her burn all night, and in the morning there she was, sunk at her dock."

"They were our last torpedoes fired in defense of Bataan," said Bulkeley. "Since December 7 we had probably sunk a hundred times our own combined tonnage in enemy warships. While we'd lost two of our six boats, neither had been hit by the enemy—both had gone aground in the dark. For every man in our combined crews, we'd already probably killed or drowned ten Japanese, and our casualties to date were only one man wounded. We were to lose more men later, and all our boats, but the Japs were to pay at almost the same ratio.

"On the way back I realized that we had fired

99

our last torpedoes, except those we would need to
fill our tubes for the run to China. And we had
just about enough gas to get us there, with hardly
a barrel to spare. If we were ever to make the run,
we must make it soon. And it was getting plain
that we couldn't do much more for Bataan, which
was on its last legs."

"I can tell you about the army," said Cox. "I
used to get bored at Sisiman Cove and take trips
to the front—sometimes up into the outposts. There
were a lot of men in uniform on Bataan, but the
front-line fighting soldiers consisted, first, of about
two thousand Americans, well seasoned and good
fighters. Then, about twelve hundred Filipino
Scouts—equally well trained and equally good.
Lastly, they had in the fighting line about twenty-
seven thousand Filipino trainees—young kids who
had never worn a uniform until a few weeks before the war started. As soldiers, they would com-
pare with American selectees who had had the
same amount of training—which is to say they
weren't worth a damn. They couldn't hit anything they shot at; if their guns jammed, they

didn't know how to fix them; and the Japanese could scare them with firecrackers—and sometimes did.

"Their officers were equally untrained. Toward the end, it was grotesque. Tough, experienced American Regular Army privates would be giving orders to Filipino generals.

"Those two thousand Americans and the twelve hundred Scouts were the only real fighting men on Bataan, and they were run ragged—every time the Japs punched a hole in the line, these experienced troops would have to be thrown in to plug it— everywhere at once.

"Then there was the item of equipment—no spare parts. They had a few tanks left, with their treads falling off. A missing fan belt would put an entire tractor out of the war—for want of a tread, a tank would be junk by the roadside.

"I drove an ambulance in France in 1940, and in some ways it was the same story on Luzon. The same lack of equipment, planes, communications. The same disorganization—everybody falling back, or maybe fighting without hope just because it was a habit. Both in France and on Luzon you threw the book away—and did what you could with what you had.

"But there were differences. In France it was 'Scram, the Germans are coming, we can't hold 'em!'—and they'd drop their arms and run.

"But on Bataan, even when they knew in their hearts it was hopeless, they'd say, 'Damn it, we're *not* backing up to Corregidor—we're going to hold them here!' They kept on fighting even down to the last ditch, when they were so tired they staggered—and I have watched them stagger—and when they surrendered, it was with their arms in their hands."

"That's more or less how it looked to us on March 1," said Kelly, "which is a day I'll never forget. It started off in a curious way—it seemed that General MacArthur wanted to take a ride on one of our boats with Bulkeley. We felt honored, but I couldn't just understand why the General would choose a time like this for a pleasure trip. Still, orders were orders, and even the air force got theirs—or rather what was left of it, which was exactly four decrepit P-40's patched together from the pieces of many others.

"This proud American air force guaranteed us air superiority over that area of the bay while the General was out on the water. The area was only four square miles, and the time only half an hour—about all the superiority this pathetic air force was able to guarantee. While the General was having his ride I was worried—suppose something had come up which might upset our dash to China? I could see the men didn't understand it either, and were starting to speculate and gossip.

"But the General explained everything when he returned from the ride, by officially presenting Bulkeley with the order decorating him with the D.S.C. We'd known about it for weeks, but this, it seemed, was the official presentation. He also congratulated the men on the fine work they had done, and handed each a package of cigarettes. It wasn't until that night that Bulkeley told me all this had been camouflage. For that morning the General had called him in and told him of the new plan. China was out for us, all right. Because Wash-

ington had made MacArthur Commander in Chief
for all the Pacific and ordered him to leave. A submarine had been suggested, but MacArthur had
said Bulkeley was the only commanding officer he
knew in whom he had complete confidence—he
was sailing with Buck. But he'd wanted to make
a trial run first, and so added the little ceremony
to allay the suspicions of the men. Because we were
leaving Bataan in absolute secrecy and very soon.

"Of course to us this meant that the China trip
—our last hope of seeing America and escaping
death or a Japanese prison—was gone forever. Now
the MTB's were like the rest here in the islands
—the expendables who fight on without hope to
the end. So far as we knew, we would now finish
up the war in the southern islands, when the Japs
got around to mopping up the last American resistance there.

"And yet I was curiously glad. Mostly, I think,
it was because of Peggy. I wasn't guilty any more.
Now we both had our duty to do here in the Philippines. Of course I would never see her again—
her job was here in Corregidor, and mine would
be down in the southern islands. But our end would

be the same. We were both expendable now. I wasn't running out on her and I felt a lot better."

"The minute we knew we were to leave Bataan soon," continued Kelly after a pause, "we got to work on the four boats. We knew the trip would be tough, and the boats were old now. The engines had had double the number of hours' service without their customary thorough overhaul and retuning, so they were making half their original speed.

"We planned to scrape the bottoms and overhaul their struts, but this was done for only three. My boat's turn was last, and meanwhile it was used for patrol.

"Overhauling those motors without any replacement parts was a terrible job. For instance. Any tank-town garage which overhauls a flivver back in the States always replaces the gaskets with new ones. Only we didn't have any. Or any sealing compound. So those old gaskets had to be carefully removed, handled as gently as though they were precious lace, and laid back in place when the motors were reassembled.

"How much gas could we carry? We experi-
mented—put down planks on those ⅜-inch plywood decks to strengthen them, and finally decided we could take a chance on piling twenty of
those fifty-gallon drums on each boat.

"Naturally the crews got curious about all these
preparations. Since we knew so much about what
the Japanese were doing across the bay, we as-
sumed their means for finding out about us were
equally good. Anyway, Bulkeley and I had decided that there is only one way of keeping a valuable secret during a war: don't tell it yourself.

"But we had to tell the men something. So we
said maybe, after we had exhausted all our gas here
on Bataan, we would head down for Cebu in the
southern islands. Cebu, where there was plenty of
food and more torpedoes, and where they had the
most beautiful and languorous girls in the islands,
and plenty of gasoline.

"We painted it as a golden spot. Only Bulkeley
and I knew that when we got to Cebu we would
be doomed—there was no gasoline there and only
a little in Mindanao. We could never hope to get
to Australia.

"But then there were the two correspondents—Clark Lee and Nat Floyd of the *New York Times*, and also Colonel Wong. They knew about the Chinese trip because the Admiral had authorized them to go with us. So we told them, yes, we were still going to China, but we didn't know when—maybe not for a long time—and advised them if they had any other chance to get out, by all means to take it. Meanwhile we kept on the boats all that landing-gear equipment we had assembled for the China trip—so if any hint of it had leaked out to the crew, they would think it was still on.

"Meanwhile MacArthur had told Bulkeley that Bataan would fall shortly, and Corregidor would go soon after—if it didn't get help from the States immediately. No help was being sent. Apparently it couldn't be gotten to us. Then the Japs could mop up the southern Philippines.

"It was a grim picture for us. But here was our last big job. MacArthur was the brains of the organization—the only general who could take that territory back. The whole allied defense depended on getting him to Australia.

"Bulkeley was reporting to him every other day, but MacArthur refused to set a date for leaving— he wanted to stay as long as he could. At this time the boys on Bataan were back in their strongest positions—also their last-ditch defense line—and the Japs had had about all they wanted monkeying with this line, and were waiting for reinforcements. But when news came that their General Yamashita was on his way with many transports, bragging he would capture MacArthur within a month, our departure date was set for March 15.

"But to keep the men occupied and also to keep our secret, we went right on with plans for developing our shore base at Sisiman Cove. We installed a good cook's galley, fixed up the mess hall, screened in everything, as though we hoped to live there for months.

"We even took all our clothes off the boats and moved them into the nipa huts ashore.

"On the fourth of March there came a nice break for me. Peggy got me word that she had been transferred to Little Baguio hospital on Bataan, relieving one of the girls who had been working too long under fire, and I got the idea of inviting her down to our base for chow and to spend the evening. Dr. Nelson, who had been looking after my hand, was also on Little Baguio, and I invited him and his girl friend, too.

"You should have seen my ship perk up when I told them. The skipper was going to bring a girl aboard! They had the ship all spit and polish, ready for the big event. My cook, Reynolds, and the Filipino mess boy were tickled pink. They were going to show the army!

"You see the week before I'd gone over to Little Baguio—I'd had only breakfast and arrived on foot late in the afternoon for my dressing, to spend the night and walk back. But they told me, regretfully of course, of a new ruling: rations were tightening—they were down to dried fish, plain rice, and one slice of bread—so absolutely no visitors could get food at the hospital. So I went to bed supperless, got up, watched them eat breakfast—they said how sorry they were they couldn't offer me any—hiked back all those miles over the hills, and at nine o'clock, sitting at our own mess table, ate seventeen hot cakes as fast as Reynolds could turn them out of the pan.

"Now their one idea was to show the army what real navy hospitality can be. It's true Peggy brought the coffee—we were out of that—but they rustled the rest. It started off with fruit cocktail, then a real pot roast of fresh meat with brown gravy, and in this a whole can of mushrooms, which they'd been hoarding for some big occasion. Then rice and canned peas and beans, a delicious apple pie, and then coffee like only we can make it in the navy. There was never such a dinner. Then we sat and talked, while the little waves lapped along the cove.

"I told Peggy I wanted to see her again, and soon. She said they were keeping her very busy, but she might get a night off on the fifteenth or before. There was no way I could call her, so she said she'd get to the signal-corps field telephone and ring me up about six o'clock on the eleventh, when we could make a definite date.

"I asked her if she couldn't make it sooner, and she said of course she wanted to, but didn't see how she possibly could. I wanted to tell her why I wanted it sooner. Then I stopped myself. Because in a war you don't tell anybody. Not anybody. And if they have any sense, and Peggy had plenty, they understand this and don't want to be told.

"So instead we talked about the war, and how they were low on quinine now—just had enough to give the worst malaria cases a light slug which would last only a short time—and how tired the soldiers were, how uncertain everything looked.

" 'It's uncertain for us in the navy, too,' I said. 'One of these days even I am liable to disappear, without telling you good-by.'

"We were silent for a minute, and then she said, sure, she realized that—she always had known it might happen. But there was no use talking about it before it came—talking didn't make anything easier. But if I did have to leave suddenly, without telling her good-by, where would I go?

" 'Almost anywhere,' I said, trying to sound vague and careless. I don't know whether it fooled her or not. But she was smart and may have guessed that either I really didn't know, or if I had orders, I should not talk about them. Anyway, after that we both sat looking out over the water in the dusk, and it was a long time before I could look at her or she looked at me."

"We were measuring out our gas drop by drop now. Our boats can use only the best 100 octane airplane grade—the same the P-40's needed. To save it I would tie my boat up to the buoy at the entrance to the mine field. A Diesel-powered launch would patrol, and only if they saw anything worth chasing would they signal us to go out and run it down. Also, MacArthur said absolutely no more offensive raids for the MTB's—he couldn't risk the boats or spare the gasoline.

"On March 10 Bulkeley made his usual trip to see MacArthur; this time he brought along all his plans and charts for the trip. The General went over and approved them, and also told Admiral Rockwell and his chief of staff that they were going along, which was the first they had known of the trip—they had thought we were going to China. There was also an ominous bit of news—some big Jap formation was reported coming down the west coast of Luzon in our direction. If it was true, it could only be the convoy bringing General Yamashita and his reinforcements. General MacArthur told Bulkeley we might be leaving very soon, and to come back the next day.

"That would be the eleventh of March. Bulkeley went over early in the morning and returned to us at noon. He called in not only me but the other officers, Akers, Cox, and Schumacher, and for the first time showed them copies of our secret orders and the charts he had worked out for our route. He made the point that we should all keep together, but if one broke down, the rest would go on, leaving it to make its way the best it could.

"If we met the enemy, we were to avoid them if possible. But if they gave chase and were gaining on us so that an attack was necessary, the 41 boat, in which he would carry the General, his wife, and his son, would turn and run, and my boat, since I was second in command, would lead the attack to give the others time to escape.

"It was an unusual situation for Bulkeley to be in. Always he had gone along on every fight and led the way, but now it couldn't be that way.

"The last thing he told us was that we were

leaving that very night. He left us hard at work on last-minute preparations but would return soon to complete his own.

"Even then we didn't tell the men what we were up to or where we were going, but they got their orders to dump that landing-force equipment, to load all spare parts on the boats, move the crew's mess gear back into the ship's galley, and pile the decks with drums of gas.

"And while we were doing it, who should walk in but Nat Floyd of the *New York Times*, exactly the last guy in the world we wanted to see. Sure, we liked him. He said he'd been up to the lines with the army, and then on a hunch, no particular reason, thought he'd drop in on us to see if we had any news. Then he kind of glanced around. What were those planks on the deck for? And all that gasoline on the wharf? Somehow the place looked a little torn up. When did we think we'd get off for China? Not for quite a while? Oh, he just asked for no particular reason, maybe because it almost looked like we were packing up—and so on. I tried every way in the world to get

114

rid of him before Bulkeley got back, but it was no use; he stuck like glue.

"Then Bulkeley and I went into a huddle. Here Nat was. And bound to get suspicious of the activity. After we'd gone, the story would be almost sure to get out.

" 'He's a pretty nice guy,' I said. 'Don't suppose we could take him with us, do you?'

" 'Well,' said Bulkeley, 'I've got to go along now. But if Nat should happen to stow away in the lazaret, and we didn't find him until we were out to sea, why then the story certainly wouldn't get out, would it?'

"And do you know, that's just what happened. But in the meantime there were other things on my mind. Mostly it was how I was going to get hold of Peggy. There was no telephone at the hospital. She'd said she would phone me sometime between six and seven o'clock today about that date of ours on the fifteenth.

"But there was a lot of traffic over that signal-corps field telephone, and she might not get to use it until almost seven. And I was due to pick up my passengers and be gone forever by 6:30 tonight.

And I'd never get to say how much I liked her and what a swell, brave kid she was, and good-by. But about seven the phone at this end would ring, and some wise-guy sergeant would answer, and tell her, no, Kelly doesn't live here any more—they've pulled out, I guess, but would anybody else do, toots?

"So I sat down and tried to write it in a letter, which I could leave at Corregidor on our way out, and which she would get when she got back from duty in the lines, and then at least would understand.

"I had just finished it about 2:30 and put it in my pocket when they came paging me for a telephone call on that signal-corps phone. It was Peggy —her duty hours had been changed, and she was afraid if she waited until seven to call I might be out on patrol, and she might miss me. She just wanted to tell me she'd been able to fix everything for our date on the fifteenth, and was that date all right with me, could I make it?

" 'No,' I said. The phone was on the wall in the Philippine army shack, and the shack was crowded with soldiers—in addition to all the guys probably listening in on the line.

"Well, she said, maybe she could change it for the sixteenth, if that would be better for me.

" 'It wouldn't be any better,' I said. 'Nothing would be any better.'

" 'Well,' she said, and she sounded a little mad, 'what is this, anyway?'

" 'I guess it's good-by, Peggy,' I said.

"Then there was a long silence, and when she spoke again I almost thought it was someone else, her voice was so changed. 'Where are you going?' she asked, very low. 'Can you tell me?'

" 'No,' I said.

" 'Can you tell me if you're coming back?'

" 'No,' I said. 'I can't tell you that.'

" 'Then I guess it's really good-by,' she said, and her voice sounded flat and a long way off. 'But it's been awfully nice, hasn't it?'

" 'Listen, Peggy, I've written you a letter—' only just then I heard the connection break. It seemed a couple of generals wanted to talk to each other. It was quite a while before I got it back again, and they told me she had waited fifteen minutes and had then gone. I've always hoped what the generals had to say to each other was important.

"Of course we weren't engaged. I didn't have a picture of her. In fact, the only thing I had was a few lines she'd scribbled on a piece of paper a few weeks before. We'd been idly talking about how we hoped to get out of the islands and agreed, half in joke, that whichever of us got out first would write the family of the other one of those reassuring letters about how wonderful life was on Bataan and how well and happy the other one had looked.

"So, half in joke, she'd scratched the address of her married sister in San Francisco on the back of an old envelope. This I still had, and I intended to write her, and send it out by the plane which took MacArthur, telling her what a swell girl her kid sister was—with more spunk in her little finger than half the men on the island."

"Kelly's 34 boat was right on time," said Bulkeley. "We in the 41 boat picked up our passengers at Corregidor and met him and the other two boats at the turning light just outside the mine field at seven o'clock to the minute. We had twenty pas-

sengers in all in our four boats. With me in the
41 boat were General and Mrs. MacArthur, their
little boy, and his nurse and a few generals. Kelly
in the 34 boat had, to start with, Admiral Rockwell, two colonels, and an army aviation captain.
When one of the other boats later broke down,
Kelly picked up a few more generals.

"But rank made no difference. Washington had
ordered MacArthur to bring out the most valuable
of his men, and so they were all specialists—there
was even a staff sergeant, who was a technician,
along with us, while thirty-odd generals were left
behind on Bataan.

"We started out single file, my boat as flagship
setting the pace for the other three. First we went
fifty miles straight out to sea in the deepening twilight. We'd hoped to get out unnoticed, but suddenly we saw a light glimmer and glow on one of
the Japanese-held islands. It was a signal fire—warning to the mainland that they'd seen us pass. If
they had seen it on Luzon, that meant trouble for
us—maybe bombers at dawn, maybe destroyers
later on in the day. By eleven o'clock we made
out the outline of Apo Island against the stars

(there was no moon) and checked our navigation, which we were doing entirely by compass and chart. MacArthur and General Sutherland were pleased with the way it was going."

"I can't say that Admiral Rockwell was," said Kelly—"maybe because he knew more about the sea than the generals did. I hadn't wanted to worry him, so I hadn't mentioned the fact that ours was the only one of the four boats which hadn't been overhauled, and was so full of carbon that we couldn't make much speed until the carbon was burned out.

"As you know, we'd intended to make a good speed, but I found my boat wouldn't quite do it. Pretty soon we were lagging fifty yards behind, then, after a while, two hundred. The Admiral didn't mention this for some time. But finally he said:

" 'Don't you think we're getting a little far apart?'

" 'We'll close in gradually,' I said. And I tried to, but finally we were so far behind Bulkeley's flagship we couldn't see it with the naked eye.

" 'Damn it,' said the Admiral. 'Let's close up!'

And he wasn't giving it just as advice any more. But I was floored as to how to achieve it. I'd been giving her all the throttle I had for the past hour. Then I had an idea.

"I sent a whispered message to the engine room, ordering them to disconnect the throttle, and to push the carburetors up with their hands as far up as they would go. We now had on every possible ounce of power, but the Admiral still wasn't satisfied.

" 'We're closing pretty slowly,' he complained.

"Privately, I doubted that we were closing at all, but I only said, 'No use pushing her too hard, sir.'

"But about five minutes later we really were closing. Bulkeley, noticing we were pretty far behind, had reduced his speed. But, with my throttles disconnected, I couldn't reduce mine, and it took me about a minute to get a message down there telling the engineers to take their hands off the carburetor levers and reconnect them with the controls on the bridge. During this minute we not only gained on Bulkeley's boat, but overtook it and went roaring madly past.

"In the darkness I could see the Admiral had squared around and was giving me a doubtful look. I could tell he thought he was riding with a madman, and I decided he would worry less if I told him the truth—that our maximum speed in this boat was something under forty knots. Any Japanese destroyer could easily make this maximum of ours, as the Admiral very well knew. But all he said was 'My God!' very softly to himself.

"It happened that we were just passing an island. The Admiral glanced over.

" 'How far are we from shore, Kelly?'

" 'About four miles, sir.'

" 'Looks farther than that to me. Take a bow-and-beam bearing.'

" 'Aye, aye, sir,' I said. But of course I didn't have any instruments. So, making the 45-degree angle with two fingers, I sighted along them to a point ahead. When we came just abeam of this point, since we knew our own speed, it would give us roughly our distance from shore—very roughly. The Admiral noticed me sighting along my fingers.

" 'Don't you have a pelorus?' he said, sharply.

" 'No, sir,' I said.

" 'H-m-m. I suppose the flagship has better means?'

" 'No, sir,' I said. 'They don't.'

" 'How in hell do you navigate?'

" 'By guess and by God, sir,' I said.

" 'My God!' said the Admiral, and this time he didn't say it so softly. 'I hope,' he added wistfully, 'that we get there.'

"And then, at four o'clock in the morning, my engines suddenly stopped. I knew the strainers were clogged with wax and rust, and it would take half an hour to clean them, which I explained to the Admiral, who was watching the other three boats disappear over the horizon.

" 'What time will we get to the rendezvous?'

"I made a fast mental calculation. 'About 8:30, sir.'

"Dawn, as we both knew, would come at seven, and with it—if the mainland had seen that island signal fire—Japanese planes, looking for us.

" 'That's an hour and a half later than I like to be out,' said the Admiral. Our plans, of course, called for running only at night, and laying up

123

by day in the Cuyo Island group, with a general rendezvous in a harbor of one of the central islands for our start at sunset.

"There are thirty or forty islands in the Cuyo group, and just before dawn we began to make out the first ones—tiny mounds on the horizon ahead and around us. The flagship had the only detailed chart of them; all I had was a large-sized map of the Philippines, and on this the Cuyos looked like a cluster of some forty-odd flyspecks.

"When the Admiral asked how in the world we —without navigation instruments or chart—expected to make a proper landfall on the particular flyspeck that we all had selected as rendezvous, I explained we had provided for that; I knew its general location, and from Bulkeley's chart I had drawn a pencil sketch of this island. But again he was skeptical.

"It was eight o'clock (no planes as yet) before we saw what we thought might be the right one; as we drew nearer, the Admiral agreed that the hills and cove were exactly like my sketch, but when we entered the cove, it was empty. We circled the island—no sign of the other three boats.

" 'My God,' said the Admiral, 'what's happened to the General? We arrive, limping in late, and the others aren't here! Where can they be?' "

"I had an idea where they would be, and I explained. Bulkeley, I was sure, would take no chances with women and a child aboard. Of course he'd seen the Japanese signal fire the night before. Planes might be out spotting us for destroyers, and as soon as dawn broke, Bulkeley undoubtedly had made for the nearest of those other Cuyos—picking one from his chart (we'd never been here before) which was surrounded by reefs and water so shallow that no destroyer could venture within gun range or even within sight. There he would wait all day, if not until dusk, at least until he thought the danger of spotting planes was past, before coming to join us here. That was my theory, and I stuck to it because it was the best one we had—the Admiral's was much more pessimistic.

"So at 8:37 we dropped a hook in the cove and I sent two men ashore with semaphore flags to climb the island's single five-hundred-foot hill and stand continuous watch—for the other three boats, of course, but particularly for Japs.

"Then we got to work gassing the ship, and it was a job. Drum by drum, we poured that 100 octane gasoline into her tanks, and it took all morning. As soon as we had entered the calm water of the cove, the army, which had been down in the cabin all night and miserably seasick, began stirring and soon showed definite signs of life—emerging into the sunlight, straightening their uniforms, and even mentioning the subject of breakfast, which wasn't unusual, considering the food that had gone overside during the night.

"We had breakfast aboard, of course, but just now it was out of the question. The ship had to be fueled at once, because no one knew when a dive bomber might chase us out of the cove. But since we feared an explosion from our highly volatile airplane gasoline, all electricity on the ship had to be turned off while we were pouring. As a result, the army got its breakfast about noon, and then there was time to look around. The island was intensely green—a few hills sloping abruptly into the sea—and our lookouts signaled down from the summit that on the other side lived nine families of natives. These had climbed the hill to gape at the Americans, and told them that the day before they had seen a big ship going south. A warship? They didn't know, but we were uneasy. The water here was deep, and a cruiser could come in fairly close.

"At 5:30, when we figured any spotting planes would have had to head back for home, I was about to pull our lookouts from the hill and get under way when they wigwagged down that they saw a ship—apparently friendly, maybe an MTB. I picked it up with my binoculars and presently made out the 32 boat, which soon tied up alongside us.

"It was this boat, remember, which had been repaired after its explosion. The cook had been blown into Sisiman Cove. During the night its struts started coming loose, so they could use only one or two of their three engines, and they, like us, had lost touch with the other boats in the night. But instead of falling far behind the flagship, they had somehow managed, in the darkness, to get out in front of it.

"In the first gray light of dawn, their stern lookout reported a strange ship—gaining on them. Looked like a Jap destroyer. Now an MTB in good condition can outrun any warship afloat. But the 32 boat was hobbling on two engines, so although he was running full throttle, its commander wasn't surprised that the strange craft kept gaining. In order to lighten his boat and pull away, he dumped six hundred gallons of gasoline in drums over the side, but still the enemy was closing on him. There seemed nothing to do now but fight before the destroyer opened with its 3-inch guns. They readied two torpedoes and turned dauntlessly for the attack, to discover just in time that the strange pursuing craft was the 41 boat—their own flagship with General MacArthur aboard.

"So here they were—loaded down to the water line with seasick and puzzled generals. Just at this point there was a rising roar from seaward, and the 41 boat came around the point, Bulkeley and General MacArthur's party."

"We'd lost sight of you a few hours before dawn," said Bulkeley, "when you stopped to clean your strainers. I went on ahead because I wanted to get as deep as possible into the Cuyo Islands before sunrise.

"As the sky pinkened I headed for the nearest and best—it was one of the prearranged crosses on the map. It wasn't much of an island—only a quarter of a mile wide—but it had plenty of shallow water to keep off Jap destroyers. We hid in the cove and stayed aboard—although we posted one lookout on the islands opposite shore. It was an untouched tropic desert islet right out of a movie travelogue. Palm trees waved lazily over a snowy white beach. The cove had a coral bottom and the water was clear as an emerald. The place was inhabited by one lone dog—a very thin one—although there were four deserted huts, to which people came once a year to collect coconuts.

"Lying at anchor, some of the crew picked off a little sleep as we rolled gently in the sunshine. Presently the General came on deck; he was a fine figure in his camel's-hair coat and gold hat, frowning a little as he squinted in the sunshine at the water and white sand. Then Mrs. MacArthur and the little boy and his Chinese amah came up to sit in wicker chairs in the sunshine. It was too bad little Arthur couldn't have played on the beach, but I told the General no one should go ashore. Because if dive bombers came over and spotted us, we would have to get the hell out of that cove quick, leaving even the lookout behind, and out into open water where we could dodge and twist. So little Arthur played with General Tojo, a dignitary who wasn't on our passenger list. He was the cook's monkey (the cook's duties also included supervising the motors and running a machine gun as well as his electric hot plate) and so Tojo more or less had the run of the ship. While Mrs. MacArthur sunned herself, the General got his exercise by pacing our little deck.

"I figured the morning would be the dangerous time for bombers, if they knew we had slipped out, so by two o'clock I felt it was safe to get under way, and we threaded down through the little shoaly channels between the islands, which would defy a destroyer or cruiser to follow, approaching the last one, which was our general rendezvous. In the distance I could see the other two boats also heading for it, and when we arrived, Kelly in the 34 boat was already there and waiting.

"Then there was the problem of what to do about the 32 boat, which had dumped most of its gas at dawn, and couldn't proceed much farther at high speed.

"This was a rendezvous not only for our four MTB's, but also for General MacArthur's second means of escape—a submarine. It had all been carefully worked out, and the submarine would bob up in this cove tomorrow. Had we been attacked or broken down, the General could have left us here, and continued his trip on down to Australia by submarine.

"Even now the General was considering taking the submarine instead. The afternoon trip had been rough, and I had to answer the General frankly that I thought the night trip would be rougher, because we would head away from the islands into the open sea. Seasickness may be a joke to sailors, but it isn't to landsmen."

"I will never forget how you looked when you pulled up alongside of us in the cove," said Kelly. "There was General MacArthur sitting on a wicker chair, soaking wet; beside him Mrs. MacArthur, also soaking wet, but smiling bravely; and then the Chinese amah holding little Arthur Mac-Arthur, both soaking wet and very seasick. You could see the Little Corporal was most unhappy but wouldn't admit it, and his jaw was set—just at the exact angle of his father's.

"Then General MacArthur, Admiral Rockwell, and Lieutenant Bulkeley talked about the night's plans—the advisability of continuing with us to-night or going by submarine. The Admiral was for staying with us, but the General was unde-cided. The afternoon trip had been rough, and Bulkeley had warned the night would be rougher. Yet as we lay there in the cove, the sea seemed calm enough, and the sky gave no hint of bad weather. So on the assurance of the Admiral that it would be good weather, the General decided they'd con-tinue with us.

"Then, as Bulkeley had said, there was the prob-lem of what to do with the 32 boat, which had dumped much of her gasoline. She did not have enough left to make the fast run with us to the island of Mindanao, where the General's party would get the plane for Australia. So Bulkeley gave her different orders. Her generals were to be transferred to my boat. She was to wait here in the rendezvous until tomorrow when the submarine arrived. She was to tell the submarine that everything had gone well, the General had gone on to Mindanao and would go to Australia by plane, as planned. Having delivered this message, the 32 boat was to go to Iloilo on the island of Panay, only one hundred and twenty miles away. There she could get repairs and enough gas to bring her on down to Cagayan to join the rest of us in the other three boats, and we would finish the war together in the southern islands.

"What went wrong with this plan, we don't know to this day. The boat's commander, Lieutenant Schumacher, must have decided that it wasn't in condition to follow these orders. Anyway, when the submarine arrived, he had it shell the 32 boat, so it would not fall into Japanese hands, and boarded the submarine, which dropped his crew off at Corregidor and took him safely to Australia.

"We found out much later that he had gotten to Australia. For some time their disappearance was a mystery, and Bulkeley here spent several days flying out over all those islands trying to find some trace of the 32 boat. Some day, of course, there will be a full report on exactly what did happen which will explain everything.

"All we know is that we last saw them back there in the cove as we left the harbor—a hard right turn and then out to sea, at about 6:30. We were leading, so that the flagship, just behind us, could search out the smoothest part of our wake, so that MacArthur's party could ride comfortably. We'd been going about fifteen minutes when the port lookout called 'Sail-ho!' and there she was —three points on our port bow, distance about five miles. 'Looks like an enemy cruiser!' said the lookout. I grabbed my binoculars, and so it was! Hull down, but masts and superstructure plain. On the course we were steering we would cross her bow. I gave the 34 full right rudder and full speed ahead—it was now much faster than eighteen knots, because the carbon had burned out of our motors. I knew that type of Jap cruiser could make thirty-five knots with all steam up. But unless they were expecting something, they could only make twenty-seven. So we had a good chance of keeping away from them—it might be dark before they could close in.

"Meanwhile I was hoping they hadn't seen us and praying that the sun would hurry up and set, but it just pooped along—seemed to hang there above the horizon for weeks, and finally bobbed under at seven o'clock.

"If you've never been in the tropics, you don't realize how fast it gets dark—almost no twilight at all."

"I think it was the whitecaps that saved us," said Bulkeley. "The Japs didn't notice our wake, even though we were foaming away at full throttle.

"During the excitement, the General was lying down in the cabin with his eyes closed, but Mrs. MacArthur, who was with him, heard everything that went on and she didn't turn a hair. She took it like a lady—went right on rubbing the General's hands to keep up his circulation, though she was seasick herself.

"I never went below, and all my men stayed at battle stations, so the people in the cabin took care of themselves—there was no one to wait on them.

The General saw that I was supplied with cigars. They were pretty well provisioned. They'd brought from Corregidor, among other things, a few cases of Coca-Cola—the first I'd tasted in many weeks—and some of the tenderest ham I ever ate.

"It got dark fast after sunset, a wind sprang up, and ahead we could see lightning flashes. But these didn't help us find the narrow passage into the Mindanao Sea. We were going in the dark entirely by dead reckoning. At midnight we figured we'd be off the strait—so we turned into the pitch-blackness, holding our breath, but still we didn't hit anything. I had no charts, I'd never been there before, I could see absolutely nothing, but since we didn't crash into a beach, we kept on going, and at last I knew we were through and safely into the Mindanao Sea—our dead-reckoning navigation had been right."

"And there we really caught hell," said Kelly. "Big foaming waves fifteen or twenty feet high thundering over the cockpit, drenching everybody topside. Also, because of the speed, water, and wind, it got damned cold. Our binoculars were full of water and our eyes so continuously drenched with stinging salt that we couldn't see, in addition to which it was pitch-black. We were making good speed through strange waters with islands all around us. We could see the outlines of the big ones—Negros and Mindanao—very dimly against the horizon through the storm. But there were dozens of small ones and probably hundreds of reefs.

"The sea was on our port bow, tending to drive us south. We expected to make a landfall forty miles dead ahead—a small island where we would turn—and let me tell you this was an unpleasant situation for a navigator. The helmsman's eyes and ours were full of salt, you had to keep one hand in front of your eyes to avoid the slapping force of the water, and yet you needed both to hold on. The Admiral was pretty wrought up. 'I've sailed every type ship in the navy except one of these MTB's,' he shouted at me above the wind, 'and this is the worst bridge I've ever been on. I wouldn't do duty on one of these for anything in the world—you can have them.'

"It was a real problem to keep a stern lookout for the 41 boat so we wouldn't lose it. Three good

waves in a row and we'd be out of sight, and in
that weather we could pass within seventy-five
yards and never see each other. The 41 was now
keeping about two hundred yards astern, hunting
for the smoothest part of our wake, to keep the
General's party comfortable. The General had said
that if his boat slowed, we who were ahead should
also slow, letting them set the pace. I know seasickness can be very unpleasant, but I wanted to
get them safe in port by dawn, in case there were
Jap planes about, so I kept pulling them on. It got
rougher and rougher, and the Admiral kept re-
membering it had been he who had assured Mac-
Arthur that Bulkeley was wrong about the weather
—it would be calm.

" 'The General's going to give me hell for this
in the morning,' he said, uneasily. 'Damned if I
thought Bulkeley knew what he was talking about
—but he surely did.'

"The Admiral stayed with me up on the bridge
the whole trip, in spite of the weather. Every half-
hour I would send a member of the crew over the
boat for inspection, to see how its hull was standing the strain, for we were taking an awful licking.

"During one of these I noticed a figure by the machine-gun turret, sitting with his feet propped up on a torpedo tube. His stomach was long ago empty, but he was leaning forward, retching between his knees. From this I guessed it might be one of our passengers, and sent a quartermaster to ask him if he wouldn't care to go below. The quartermaster returned and saluted: 'The general says he doesn't want to move, sir—he knows what's best for him.'

"It was now about three in the morning. I'd had no sleep for two days and two nights and could do with a little coffee, so I sent Lieutenant Brantingham below for the thermos jug, and also to take a look at any of our passengers who might care for a little refreshment.

"Brantingham returned with three cups of coffee—stone-cold but plenty strong, and it took the salt taste from our mouths—and reported none of the passengers had accepted his invitation.

" 'Where are they?' I asked.

" 'Two generals and a colonel are in the forward compartment lying on the deck. They seemed unhappy,' Brantingham reported.

" 'But why doesn't someone offer them a bunk?' I asked.

" 'Sir,' said my radio man, 'I offered one general my bunk after I'd stepped on him in the dark, but he said, "Son, just leave me be. I haven't got the strength to move." So I figured they knew what they wanted and left.'

"Four o'clock was the zero hour for all of us. I was terribly cold myself, and looking at the Admiral I could see his teeth were chattering. Yet he was a tough old sailor, and wouldn't think of leaving—here he was, in his fifties, taking a beating which would put under many men in their twenties. But I insisted he let me get him a sweater—it would be soaking in thirty seconds, and yet might do him some good. When I went down to hunt for it, I stepped on something soft and produced a groan; it turned out I had gone over my shoe tops into the soft abdomen of a general. But while I was getting my flashlight turned on to see what it was, I managed to step on another general, who was too weak even to groan. I don't think he cared if he lived or died. The only person enjoying the trip was an air-corps captain. You can no more make one of them seasick than you can a sailor. He was snoring in his bunk, happy as a baby.

"Shortly thereafter we were supposed to make a landfall—an island about half a mile square, at which point we must turn in order to make the final landfall which would bring us into port.

"With such a wind and sea, we were probably retarded, but by how much? I had to guess at it. Also the helmsman was having a wrestling match with the wheel—it was all he could do to keep within ten degrees on either side of the compass course—which meant a possible error of twenty degrees. We missed the island entirely in the dark, and from then on until dawn I changed course as I thought necessary. Dawn came at six and we saw land ahead, a point which I thought was the peninsula just west of Cagayan, our destination. I showed it to the Admiral, and he shook his head with satisfaction.

" 'Good navigation, Kelly,' he said. 'I wouldn't have believed it possible.' But it was beginning to calm down now—we could open up to thirty knots, and our passengers began to show a restored

interest in life, getting up off the floor and straightening their rumpled uniforms for entering port.
The Admiral and I on the bridge were presently
visited by an air-corps general, who looked around
and told us he was sure we were lost.

" 'Have you ever been to Cagayan before, General?' asked the Admiral.

" 'Flown over it twice. That point ahead there
is sixty miles to the west of Cagayan.'

"'I'd never been there before, but I was fairly
sure of my navigation. Also I'd spent the night
peering at what few landmarks there were—not
lying on the floor. Anyway I wasn't going off on
any tangents, investigating someone else's ideas,
so I stuck to my story.

"But now the Admiral was doubtful again.
'Kelly, I'm going to take back what I said. I'll say
it's a nice landfall when we tie up—if we ever do.'

"We were up to top speed now, carbon burned
from the motors, and at 6:30 we sighted the light
on the point at Cagayan's entrance. We slowed to
let the 41 boat lead the way, as it had the channel
charts."

"General Sharp, commanding officer of the

island of Mindanao, was down there to meet us, and as soon as we could see the pier we woke up General MacArthur," said Bulkeley. "He shook the salt water out of his gold general's cap, flipped it on his head—somehow it always lands at a jaunty angle, seems to go with his cane—and looked around with his jaw set—a fine figure of a soldier.

"Then he said to me, 'Bulkeley, I'm giving every officer and man here the Silver Star for gallantry. You've taken me out of the jaws of death, and I won't forget it!'

"Still later that afternoon he told me: 'If the boats never accomplish anything more and were burned now, they'd have earned their keep a thousand times over. If possible, when I get to Melbourne I'll get you and your key men out.'

"We arrived on the thirteenth. Four flying fortresses from Australia were supposed to have met the General. One cracked up on the take-off, two came down in the Australian desert, and the one which finally arrived had supercharger trouble and had to turn around and go back without any passengers, so MacArthur didn't get away until the eighteenth.

"We told the crews to keep quiet, not to let it get out whom we'd brought in, so the Japs wouldn't find out and maybe attack while Mac-Arthur was waiting."

"The afternoon we arrived," said Kelly, "Bulkeley told us what MacArthur had said about getting us out if he could. It was good news, but we weren't exactly excited. For if the air force couldn't get even one serviceable plane up here from Australia to take MacArthur out, what chance had we?

"Our job, I knew, would be to fight out the war in the southern islands—with torpedoes while we had them, and on land with rifles when they were expended. So better not get our hopes up.

"The boats were to be anchored off the beach, and before I left mine, I told my executive officer to check on the anchor—we were close to the beach and there was a lot of surf pounding the coral. Just to make doubly sure, I went on the forecastle for a last inspection myself. The line seemed taut. I tugged to make sure, and it came loose in my hand.

" 'Start the engines immediately!' They were

144

started in thirty seconds, but five seconds later there was a grinding scrape—one propeller had hit bottom. The other engine conked out, and when we did get it going it was too late, the waves were slapping at us broadside, each breaker driving us farther and farther on the beach.

"I yelled over to the 41 boat to get under way and give us a tow, but by the time we'd tied her line onto ours, we were stuck—hard and fast. We worked furiously four hours until the tide had gone out, and by midnight we were solid as concrete, in water so shallow that now there were only three feet of water aft and less than a foot forward. Impossible to get off that night. I went to bed disgusted.

"Next morning I was up at five and there she was high and dry except for six inches of water at her stern, and a crowd of natives gawking. It all happened because the anchor shackle had parted— the threads stripped. It was the old story—continuous usage and no replacement of parts.

"Since the MTB's didn't have the power to get us off, I finally found a sergeant in charge of an army launch powered by a ninety-horse-power Japanese Diesel and asked him for a tow. High tide was at 8:30. The little launch strained, puffed—lines parted—and at ten o'clock it broke off the tug's towing post entirely, so that was out.

"Sunday, we were again up at dawn. We had persuaded the army to lend us a sergeant and a working party of native troops, and we started digging and pounding away at the coral the propellers and rudders had chewed into.

"Bulkeley came around at 7:30. 'Frankly, Kelly,' he said, 'you'll have a hell of a time to get her off. I'm afraid we'll have to blow her up if the enemy comes. She's certainly done her part, but this may be the end. I've got to go to Del Monte. However, keep working. It's up to you.'

"I called the crew into the forward compartment and told them the skipper had left it up to us. I talked about what the old boat had done to date with them in it—sunk two ships and two landing boats. So now, were we going to let this be her end—sit by and watch the surf pound her to pieces? Or were we going to get her off?

" 'You're damn right we're going to get her off!' they said, and someone suggested maybe we could hire work gangs of natives to help us, whereupon the whole crowd started pulling money out of their pockets and piling it on the table. They'd had no pay since the start of the war, but since they'd been down here in Mindanao, they'd had shore leave and a chance to play poker with the army. The government could cut the cost of the war by just paying the army and then giving the sailors a chance to play poker with them.

"We hired what men we could, and all of us got to work with them digging out those razor-sharp coral boulders with our naked hands. But there were other boulders fifty yards out. We got some dynamite and worked all one afternoon pounding holes in them and blowing them up. With our money we hired natives driving carabao to pull pieces away, at the rate of one peso for the native and another for the carabao.

"We were about ready now for the test. Another army tug showed up. We hitched a line onto it, we bridled the wheelhouse of the first tug with a line, and as the tide came in we took soundings. The 34 boat needed five feet of water to float—

that meant we'd had to dig a two-foot hole under her—had we done it?

"High tide was nine o'clock at night. At 8:45 the two tugs started a steady pull; she didn't budge. The water churned as we took soundings. As nine approached, we signaled the tugs to give everything they had. At 9:03 the 34 gave a sudden lurch —she was free and would fight once more! But first something had to be done about her back end —rudders, struts, and propellers were a jumble of bent steel.

"Before he left for Del Monte the skipper had told us he'd heard of a little machine shop up the coast at Anaken which might possibly have tools to straighten our steel if by some miracle we got her free. So we begged a tug from an army colonel to tow us up there. We were gone ten days, and I missed one of the high spots of the whole campaign while we were gone."

"It wasn't much," Bulkeley insisted. "Just one of those things where they thank you if you do it, but give you hell if you fail. The army called me in and said that President Quezon was over on Negros Island, and if he could be brought over here, they hoped to get him out to Australia by plane. The trip to Negros was risky—seven Jap destroyers were loose in the vicinity. Probably to cut off Quezon's escape. So they weren't going to order it. They weren't even asking it. They were just explaining to me. But of course I knew they hoped for it.

"So we left at seven o'clock—I was in the 41 boat and Akers was commanding the 35. Off Apo Island, we sighted one Jap destroyer, but luckily she didn't see us and we could dodge around the island in time. It was one o'clock when we entered Dumaguete—it was pitch-dark; both the town and the harbor were blacked out. We had no chart—I'd never been there before—and when we pulled up to the pier—no President! However, his aide, Major Soriano, was there to meet us. He said three hours ago, after we had already left Mindanao, Quezon had got a telegram from General Wainwright ordering him to cancel the trip—there were so many Jap craft in the neighborhood it was too risky. But Soriano said as long as I was here, maybe we could go over to the President's home—it was about forty-five kilometers away—and he might change his mind. We went ripping over there in Soriano's car at sixty miles an hour. Quezon was up, dressed, and considerably interested. He listened to us, looked me over very carefully—I had a long black beard then, which must have been quite impressive—and finally said he'd go. (Later on when he saw me in Melbourne, shaved, he said he'd have never disregarded Wainwright's orders if he'd known he was riding with a mere child of thirty.) Anyway, Quezon and his family were loaded into cars and we were off. So then we started for the dock.

"Meanwhile I'd left Akers on patrol outside the harbor. If a Jap destroyer came nosing around, I didn't want him to cut off our retreat and figured Akers could handle him."

"I was riding back and forth, about two miles offshore in my 35 boat," said Akers, "keeping my eyeballs peeled for any of these seven Jap destroyers, when all of a sudden there was a thud and a splintering noise—we had crashed into a submerged object, a raft with metal on it apparently, which ripped a twenty-foot strip out of our bow. Water came pouring in, and we got busy with buckets and pump—"

"—and kept right on with your patrol—" said Bulkeley—"which took plenty of guts."

"The water kept gaining on us, but we thought we could hold it until Bulkeley got back with Quezon to the pier, although I knew we could never get her back to Mindanao in that condition. When I saw the lights of the car I figured it was safe to come into the harbor. She was sinking fast then, so we left her in a place where she would drift on the sand and in the morning the army could salvage her machine guns. Then we all climbed aboard the 41 boat with Bulkeley and the Quezon party. You might say that was the end of the 35 boat, and yet it wasn't quite, although she'd fought her last fight. Bulkeley was working frantically to keep the squadron together. A few days later he came over, plugged the hole temporarily, and towed her back to Cebu, where we hoisted her on the marine railway for repairs. We burned her just before the Japs came into the town."

"The trip back with Quezon was as rough as I'll ever see," said Bulkeley. "We left at three

151

o'clock with one hundred twenty miles to go before dawn. At four o'clock a big sea landed us a punch in the jaw which knocked two torpedoes loose in their tubes and instantly they started a hot run—a terrific hissing of compressed air, the propellers grinding, it sounded like the end of the world.

"In a situation like that," said Bulkeley, "the logical thing is to get them out by firing an impulse charge—touch off some black powder in the rear of the tube which sends them scooting. But we were having trouble with the mechanism—it took a minute to get this done, and meantime the two aft torpedoes were sticking out of the tubes so far they seemed about to fall, so the two torpedomen, Houlihan and Light, got out on them with their feet, hanging on by their hands to the forward tubes, and tried to kick them loose. They couldn't, but they certainly impressed President Quezon, who, when he got to Australia, gave them the Distinguished Conduct Star of the Philippines for what they did that night, as well as to Ensign Cox and me. And it was a ticklish job for the torpedomen too. Before we blew the torpedoes out, their back ends, where their motors are, turned pink and then bright red from the heat. On a normal run, of course, the surrounding water keeps them cool. But out of the water, they're not nice things to crawl around on.

"At first President Quezon didn't understand what was going on, and asked why we were getting ready to fire the two torpedoes. Not wanting to worry him unnecessarily, I said we were just firing them at the enemy, who was near by. When we got him ashore at Oroquieta, I explained that we'd really been in quite a dangerous situation.

"We found a passage through the coral reef outside Oroquieta just at dawn and found General Sharp waiting in his car. In order not to be recognized, Quezon tied a red bandanna over his face below his eyes. But the natives all knew him in spite of it—hats were waving from the sidewalk as he rode off down the street."

"We missed it all," said Kelly, "because we were up there in Anaken trying to repair the crumpled steel in our hind end at that little oversize garage back among the bamboo which they called a machine shop. Native divers, holding their breath, took off the struts and shafts of the rudders and the propellers. We tried to pound the propellers back into shape with hammers on palm logs, while the proprietor did his best to straighten the rest in his machine shop.

"He was a nice guy, but he regarded us with mixed emotions. In one way he was glad to have us there, because if the Japs attacked by sea we could be most useful. On the other hand, if their planes saw us, they might blow his setup to hell trying to paste us. And he was doing a lot of good work for the army. The longer we stayed, the more unpopular we got.

"Finally there was a trial run. She'd make only 12 knots—a fraction of her normal speed—and the vibration was terrible; you'd think someone had packed an earthquake in our lazaret.

"At about this time the skipper showed up. He told us about the trip for Quezon and the damage to the 35 boat, which he had towed into Cebu for repairs. He was still out hunting for the 32 boat, which hadn't been seen since he left it to rendez-vous with the submarine on the MacArthur trip, and he had one-third of the entire American air force of the southern Philippines out combing the island channels for her. One-third of this American southern Philippine air force consisted of exactly one Beechcraft commercial pleasure plane, which when war started had been commandeered from a civilian, and an army major who flew Bulkeley around in it. The other two-thirds were a wheezy P-40 and a very tired P-35. Bulkeley risked his neck for days in this search, not knowing, of course, that the 32 boat had been sunk and her commander was now safely en route to Australia.

"The skipper was frantic to get some of our little fleet back into commission so we could finish out the fight. We'd started the war with six boats. Two were lost off Bataan. One was lost on the escape trip south. That left only three, and two of these were wrecks, fit only for the dry dock, Bulkeley's being the only craft left in fighting condition. But he was bound to get the others back into shape. Did I think I could get mine to Cebu? It was the second largest city in the Philippines and they had a real machine shop—no dry dock but a marine railway, one of those contraptions where a track goes down the beach into the sea. You load the boat onto a small car and winch it up the track.

"Well, we could try, and we started off, my poor old boat with her earthquake making twelve knots, her back end wiggling like a shipwrecked sailor's dream of a French musical-comedy star. Whatever she was good for now, it wasn't fighting, and I was glad we didn't meet any Japs.

"The machine shop was run by 'Dad' Cleland, a seventy-one-year-old American who'd been in the islands since 1914, and a swell gent he was— originally from Minnesota and a typical hulking frontiersman. Didn't look a day over fifty and was a kind of patriarch in those parts. His native name meant 'the old man' or 'the head man' in Tagalog.

"He was a great gourmet, too. Had Bulkeley and me out to dinner and we had bottled beer (a great rarity), a big crab-meat cocktail, and then lobster Newburg, which was delicious, but 'Dad' kept warning us to hold back, because then he broke out a couple of roast ducks. 'Dad' and I divided the biggest duck between us and had all we could hold. The skipper here, on account of his rank, rated a duck all to himself, but he foundered and couldn't finish it. On the side there were canned asparagus and corn, pickles, and sweet potatoes.

"Dessert was simple, like the last bars of a symphony. Just delicious chilled mangoes and Chase & Sanborn's coffee. It was a magnificent feed after the native chow I'd been eating. We talked about the war. People in Cebu felt the show was about up, unless miraculous help arrived soon.

" 'What are you going to do when the Japs come?' we asked 'Dad.' He straightened up—all six feet two of him.

" 'Have my dignity to think about,' he said. 'I'm not going to the hills. I'll stay right here and face them. They can get me if they can, but they'll have a fight on their hands first.'

" 'Dad' was working for the government for a dollar a year. When he finally finished with our repairs—they took many days—we asked him how much the bill was. 'We'll forget about it,' he said. 'You fight 'em and I'll fix 'em. It's the least I can do.'

"He clenched his big fist, and it was about the size of a nail keg. Since I've come back here I've read about some outfits working on war contracts who were paying their stenographers fifty thousand dollars a year and charging it to the government as expenses until they were caught. It's a waste of time to indict them. Just get old 'Dad' Cleland back here and let him go in and reason with them in their swivel chairs. With those big fists of his, he'd know how to expostulate with racketeers like that.

"Until we got to Cebu we hadn't been paid since the war started. Well, in Cebu the men all got paid and it was quite a spectacle. The dozen on my boat, going from bar to bar, got rid of two thousand dollars in three days. If it had been two million instead, they would have got rid of it just as quick, although it might have strained them some. Then they settled back to their routine means of livelihood, which was playing poker with the army.

"But things were moving in Cebu, and very secretly we began to hear hints of a big American offensive which was coming rolling up from the south through the islands in time to save Bataan, which was almost out of food and ammunition. Word came that two submarines were arriving in Cebu, where they would be loaded with food and returned to Bataan—we brought the first one in through the channel

"It was a big secret—the area was cleared for two miles around. The loading was done at night and by officers only—we helped until our hands were raw—because they were fearful that some sailor or soldier might drop a hint of it in a native bar where it would get to the Japs. For three solid nights we worked until my back and arms ached, stowing all that stuff in the subs, but all the time I kept thinking of Peggy and the grand old gang up there on the Rock and what was left of the peninsula—fighting on without hope or food. Well, here was a little of both we were sending them. To make more room they stripped the submarines of torpedoes—gave 'em to us, four for the 35 boat if we could ever get her into action, two for the 41 boat, which already had two, and charged them for us with compressed air from the submarine's tanks. Now the MTB's were ready for battle, and into the submarine's empty tubes we stuffed food, and I kept thinking, as we shoved it in—there's another square meal for Peggy back there on the Rock.

"But that wasn't half of it. Because in addition to the subs—the last one shoved off on April 5—there were seven fat interisland steamers being secretly loaded with food down near 'Dad' Cleland's dock—medical supplies, quinine the boys were dying without, everything they needed to hold on. But how could they hope to get these fat little tubs up through the islands to Bataan? Bulkeley was to find out three days later."

"The General in command at Cebu called me in and verified the hints we'd heard of the big American offensive," said Bulkeley. "He assured me everything was set. It was to start at dawn the very next morning. That very night, twelve fortresses and heavy bombers were coming up from Australia. A swarm of P-35's were on their way up from Mindanao to Iloilo, where they were to gas up and go into action.

"The bombers were to land at Mindanao, gas up, take off, and blow the be-Jesus out of every

Jap warship in the region, and meanwhile the convoy of interisland steamers would start for Bataan, bringing food enough for weeks. Bataan was to be saved after all.

"The General showed me messages from all the other generals who commanded in different islands, co-ordinating the offensive. But there was one minor hitch, he explained.

"Aerial reconnaissance had spotted a couple of Jap destroyers steaming down the coast of Negros Island. Somewhat to the eastward there was a cruiser which carried four seaplanes, but they weren't worried about it. But that afternoon reports had come in giving the progress of the Jap destroyers. Obviously they were heading toward Cebu. Maybe they had broken down our American codes and knew about the interisland steamers, and were coming in either to blockade them or to shell them at the dock.

"Why couldn't we have a part in this great offensive which tomorrow was to sweep up and blast Jap shipping and warships between Mindanao, Cebu, and Bataan? We could be helpful by going out tonight and knocking off one or both of those

Jap destroyers, which by midnight should be approaching the narrow channel between Cebu and Negros islands. The cruiser—never mind her, American bombers would polish her off in the morning."

"Bulkeley came in at eight o'clock that night and told me about it," said Kelly. "My boat had been in the water just four hours—she was supposed to soak for twenty-four before she should be exposed to any pounding, but I asked him if we couldn't go out with him. 'I was hoping you'd like to,' the skipper told me. 'Think you can make it?' 'I don't know,' I said, 'but we'll soon find out. This'll be as good a dock trial for her as any.'"

"To man the boats I called for volunteers," said Bulkeley. "I had no trouble about that. I guess they understood by now that any man who doesn't volunteer won't be in the squadron long if I can get rid of him."

"They were all tickled to be in on the big offensive," said Kelly. "It was apparently so well prepared that the army had given us the radio frequency of the co-ordinating planes—that big American air umbrella which would be spread over us at dawn—in case we needed to talk with them."

"We got out to the island passage about 11:30 that night and sneaked in close to shore," said Bulkeley. "The moon wasn't due until 2:30. I was riding in the 41 boat, Ensign Cox commanding, while Kelly had his 34 boat. We'd worked out our strategy. If two destroyers showed up, my boat was to tackle the leading one and Kelly the second. If only one arrived, my boat would attack her on the quarter, and Kelly's on the bow.

"At five minutes to twelve Glover, the quartermaster at the wheel, called 'Look—there she is!' A black object was coming round the point. 'Jumping Jesus!' said Glover. 'There she is!'—because it was no little Jap destroyer but a thundering big Kuma class cruiser sliding around that point—so clear we could almost make out her 6-inch guns. She was loafing along at about ten knots.

"I gave our boat a hard right rudder, sneaking in toward the shore where the cruiser couldn't see us. Apparently she was alone. Now we curved out, into firing position, on her port beam, making as little noise as we could, and as she passed, five hundred yards away, Cox fired two torpedoes, but they straddled her."

"We fired two from our side," said Kelly, "but they also missed."

"After that," said Ensign Cox, "we in the 41 boat made a wide arc and attacked again with our last two torpedoes—Bulkeley himself firing them, and this time two of them hit, right under the bridge. They made no flash, but a good bump and a column of water. But even before that the cruiser had waked up—probably saw the wakes of one of the torpedoes—anyway she speeded up to twenty-five knots and her searchlight came on and she waved it wildly around in the air, probably looking for torpedo planes."

"Our torpedoes were all gone in the 41 boat," said Bulkeley, "but I turned around and ran astern of the cruiser to draw her fire so Kelly could get in for his second attack. Then we saw the destroyers, but they wouldn't give chase, although I tried to create the illusion of a lot of boats by firing machine-gun tracers."

"When the cruiser's searchlight came on," said Kelly, "I turned right to cross her wake and came in on her other quarter. She picked me up astern with her lights and began banging away at me with her secondary batteries—50-calibers and 40-millimeter guns—from about twelve hundred yards. The stuff was going right over our heads in a continuous stream of fire.

"But I was good and mad because our first torpedoes had missed," said Kelly, "so I decided to chase her. I told one machine-gunner to fire at her searchlight, which was blinding me, and the others to sweep her decks to get her gun crews.

"After a few minutes' chase, we had closed in to three hundred yards, so close that her searchlight seemed to be coming right down on us from an angle—about like the sun in mid-afternoon. Then I drew out onto her starboard quarter and fired our last two torpedoes—an overtaking shot. They were the last two our squadron was to fire in the war.

"Then I gave the boat a hard right rudder and started running away—for we were defenseless now except for our machine guns. But the rain of Jap tracers kept right on, and suddenly another Jap ship showed up fifteen hundred yards away.

Both started firing their main batteries at me and we were trapped between—splashes all around us now, as close as twenty-five yards. We started zigzagging wildly, trying to dodge the two searchlights, and also the streams of fire which were crisscrossing above our heads like wicker basketry, and landing in the water all around us. It seemed like weeks, but was probably only a few seconds. My junior officer, Ensign Richardson, had the wheel, while I was watching the cruiser through my binoculars. Suddenly I saw a big splash and detonation in the middle of her belly—another two seconds, another splash and detonation right in her engine room! Our overtaking shots had both hit home! Her searchlight went from bright yellow to orange to red to dull brick-red and finally winked out. Every gun stopped firing. She was jet-black now.

"But I didn't have much time for philosophizing, because this other destroyer was on my starboard bow, closing in, banging away with her 5½-inch guns and me with only 50-caliber machine guns left."

"Kelly got twenty-three salvoes of 5½-inch

steel that night," said Bulkeley, "but there was no doubt that his two torpedoes polished off the cruiser. I saw her searchlight fade out, and heavy yellow smoke arise. Her stern was under in three minutes—the destroyer put the searchlight on her decks, where the Japs were all running around, not knowing where to go—and she had sunk in twenty.

"But I was running around with three destroyers after me, which were firing all they had, and I could see another one hot on Kelly's tail. That was the last I could see of him and I thought he was a goner.

"My destroyers chased me down to Misamis, but at dawn I dove into a place to hide—there were six miles of shallow water where they couldn't follow even if they had seen me. We spent the day sleeping."

"They didn't get us then," said Kelly. "At midnight our escape began. The destroyer lost me with its light temporarily, so I did a ninety-degree turn so as to pass astern of her and lose her. I continued on that course five minutes, heading directly away from her, then to the left in another ninety-degree turn, and I started looking around the ship.

"I found Reynolds, my port gunner (he was also cook), had been shot through the throat and shoulder. I got him down below and had the chief torpedoman and the radioman give him first aid.

"I found our mast had been shot off a foot over my head, so we couldn't use our radio for sending. The port turret had been hit and its guns were out of action.

"Our objective now was to get Reynolds to a doctor. We were going like a bat out of hell. I couldn't see the 41 boat—it was so dark I couldn't even see the shore. I just had to look at the compass and make mental estimates as to how far we had gone in various directions since I last had seen land I recognized, and then guess where we now were. I thought we were near the narrow channel between the islands; would another Jap destroyer be laying for me there?

"Suddenly, directly ahead, a searchlight came on, less than a mile away—a Jap steaming full speed at me. I barely had time to give a hard left and a hard right and we went scooting past each other at a relative speed of sixty knots before he had a chance to fire a shot. He turned, holding me down with his light like a bug under a pin, and started chasing, blazing away with big guns—two splashes four hundred feet away, two more fifty feet away. I started zigging to squirm out of that light— wouldn't let my gunners fire a shot; it would help him keep our position. I was getting away, all right, but he kept firing for ten minutes, although his accuracy was going to hell. By 1:30 I could barely see his light, which was waving around, searching the water back of us.

"I kept on, wide-open, wondering how we'd ever get in, since we had no charts, it was black as pitch, and I knew coral reefs must be all around us. At four o'clock I slowed down and headed into where I hoped the beach was, taking soundings. The water suddenly shoaled off and bump! we were aground—a pinnacle of coral under our belly. Looking down with flashlights we could see the water was twenty feet deep with coral pinnacles all around us about every twenty feet, like a petri-fied forest, rising to within five feet of the surface.

"Studying the shore line, I realized we were

about ten miles too far up the coast. I sent Ensign Richardson ashore in a rowboat to send an army doctor and ambulance out from Cebu for Reynolds, and also a tug for us.

"For the next hour we sallied ship—rocking it, trying to jiggle it off the pinnacle, backing with the engines—and finally managed to roll it off. We backed carefully out of that petrified submarine forest—it was five o'clock now—and started looking for the channel entrance. Since we had no charts, it had to be guesswork and guessing had proved dangerous, so I decided to lay to out there in the open sea, waiting for dawn.

"And why not? Didn't we have air superiority now? I hoped with luck that maybe we'd see some of the big squadrons which had roared up from Australia during the night, and would spend the day pounding Jap shipping and warcraft. Well, they needn't bother about the cruiser—we'd attended to her.

"Reynolds was feeling fine now. I'd suddenly remembered a little present Peggy had given me on the Rock, went down to my locker and brought it up for him—a couple of codeine tablets and a sedative pill. Now he was sitting topside smoking, although he couldn't drink because the water would leak out the hole in his throat. They'd been short of drugs on the Rock, but she sneaked these out for me just in case I got wounded out on patrol. A hell of a thoughtful present, and much more valuable and useful than a gold cigarette case.

"Well, tonight we'd helped pay her back. The cruiser was out of the way, the planes would be here any minute, to put the destroyers on the run. Presently the seven fat little intercoastal steamers, loaded deep with supplies, would be waddling up the coast so Bataan could hold on. It looked like a good war now. Of course our torpedoes were all gone and you could technically say we were expended. But we had plenty of fight left, and if the tide of war had really turned, there would be more torpedoes and gasoline.

"Dawn came with a low fog which shut out the coastal contours, and because of all the coral we had to stand well off the coast. The sun was well up but that didn't worry me; with air superiority we didn't need to skulk in the dark any more. By 7:30 the sun had burned the fog away and we started out on two engines—one screw had banged up on the coral but that didn't matter—we were crippled now, but 'Dad' Cleland would quickly fix us. At eight o'clock we spotted the entrance to the long channel and turned in.

"So there we were, fat, dumb, and happy, heading up the narrow channel at fifteen knots, when all of a sudden—Wham! It was a hundred-pound bomb which landed about ten feet off our bow. It blew a hole into the crew's washroom you could walk through. It tore the port machine gun off its stand. It blew all the windshields in—and covered us with water and mud.

"What did I think? Well, I remember what I said. Before even I looked up, I yelled, 'Those crazy bastards, don't they know we're on *their* side?'

"Then I looked up, and here a second plane was peeling off, coming out of a cloud. But instead of the big white stars of the American air corps on her wings, there were the flaming suns of Japan!

"I didn't have time even to wonder what in hell had become of our big American offensive and the air umbrella, because I had to throttle back, stopping the boat momentarily so that the next bomb would land twenty-five feet in front instead of squarely on us. Then I gave her the gun and started trying to zigzag in that narrow four-hundred-foot-wide channel, meanwhile giving word to our machine guns to start firing.

"They bombed us for thirty minutes, and the farthest bomb was thirty feet away. We would wait for the bomb release, see it start falling, then I'd give hard rudder and it would miss by a few feet. All the while we had to keep in this narrow channel so we wouldn't be beached helplessly on a coral reef, and work our way down it toward port, where presently some of the newly arrived American planes would see what was going on and come to help. We didn't doubt, of course, that they'd arrived. Four Jap seaplanes were after us, working in rotation—undoubtedly those from the second cruiser the army had reported as being around.

"When their bombs were exhausted they began diving down just over our mast stub to strafe us. With their first salvo they killed Harris. He was my torpedoman and also manning the starboard

50-caliber machine guns—a fine kid he was—he slumped down from his guns and rolled on the deck when a bullet ripped into his throat. So I put in Martino, or started to, but found they had also hit the gun and put it out of action.

"But meanwhile Ross, with the starboard 30-caliber machine guns, had shot down one of the four planes. The next plane got Ross in the leg, and also put out his gun. So we now had no guns, only two engines and a boat full of holes with three planes diving down to less than one hundred feet, raking us with fire which we couldn't return—only try to dodge.

"The engineer now reported the engine room was full of water and the boat was sinking, so there was nothing to do but beach her, if we were to save the wounded men. I headed her over towards nearby Kawit Island, and there she beached, hard and fast. There were about twelve hundred yards of shallow surf, four feet of water over an uneven bottom of coral and sand, and then the palms. The planes kept up their strafing as we lay there, but there was nothing to do now but dodge while we got the wounded ashore.

"I went down into the engine room and there was Hunter, my chief machinist's mate, with his arm practically blown off—a bullet had entered his elbow and gone out a three-inch hole in his fore-arm, but he was still manning the engines. I gave the order to abandon ship. It turned out that there were only three of us unhit, so it was a job getting the wounded out while the Japanese dived to rake us. We made the mistake of taking off our shoes, and the coral cut our feet to ribbons as we stag-gered carrying the men.

"I found Reynolds, who had been wounded in the throat during the night, now lying with his hand over his belly.

" 'Mr. Kelly,' he said, 'leave me here.'

" 'What happened?' I asked.

" 'When the planes attacked,' he said, 'there didn't seem to be anything for me to do, so I went below and lay down on Mr. Brantingham's bunk. They hit me in the belly while I was lying there. I'm done for, sir. I'll be all right here. You get out the others.'

"Well, the hell with that. So in spite of his pro-tests, Martino and I carried him ashore. Then we

175

went back for a last trip. Only Harris was left, lying where he had tumbled into the tank compartment. But the radioman and I carried his body ashore, because we hoped to give him a decent burial.

"Then I rounded up some native soldiers, who got stretchers, and in these we carried the wounded to the other side of the island where they could be loaded into a launch, putting them in charge of Sheppard, a first-class machinist's mate, to get them to the hospital.

"At this point a banca showed up, and in it was a native doctor, the one we had sent Ensign Richardson ashore for, before dawn, for Reynolds, who by now was en route to the hospital. So I loaded the ship's papers, binoculars, and stuff into this banca, and with them I shoved off for Cebu.

"Halfway over the three planes came back and we tried to hide behind a fish trap—a net with bamboo poles sticking up out of the water. But they weren't strafing now. They were looking for the fourth plane we'd shot down. They scoured the area for twenty minutes. After they left we went on in, and of course I went straight to army headquarters, and met the colonel in charge—the No. 2 officer of the island. No, he hadn't heard from Bulkeley, but he'd send out a radio message to hunt for him if he was still alive. And maybe I'd better give my report direct to the general. I wanted to, and also I wanted to find out what had happened to our big American offensive we had been asked to be part of, and that air umbrella which should have protected us this morning.

"The general had been having a conference at the bar of the American Club, sitting with some other officers and some civilians who were now all having a drink. Now a general is pretty important, and you don't just go barging into his conferences —not if you're a mere naval lieutenant in command of a little seventy-foot boat. So, following the lead of this conducting colonel, we stood off a bit and waited until the general gave us the signal to come on in and tie up at his table. He saw us all right, but he didn't give us the signal—just went on talking to the other officers and civilians.

"Now, thinking back, I realize it was a most important conference. But at the time I was excited, because I had just come from my boat in which I'd fought all through the war and with which we'd just helped to sink a Jap cruiser—my boat which was now lying beached across the bay, with one man dead, another dying, and all the rest but three wounded. I suppose I was unstrung. I wanted to have him make my report by radio about the cruiser. And then, although maybe it wasn't my business, I'd have liked to find out about that American offensive he'd invited us to join the night before.

"We kept standing there, the two of us, while I got madder and madder. I see now it was unreasonable, but I couldn't help it then. Finally it embarrassed even the colonel and he invited me to step over by the bar and have a drink with him. I said no, thanks, I had work to do, but I'd have a Coca-Cola. I stuck around ten more minutes drinking it and then, since the general gave us no signal, I shoved off.

"I arranged to have the boat guarded. Because I wouldn't yet admit that maybe both it and we were expended now. High tide was at four o'clock. Couldn't we maybe patch her up, float her over to 'Dad' Cleland's, get torpedoes and a crew from somewhere, and maybe fight her just once again?

"I went over there to where Brantingham and the 35 boat were, taking the stuff I'd salvaged from the boat, and they gave me some lunch as I talked about the fight and what had happened to us, and during it Ensign Richardson telephoned. He said Reynolds had died, and they were burying him and Harris in the American cemetery with a military escort and a priest, at four o'clock. I said of course I would go, and would meet Richardson at the bar of the American Club, from which we'd go over together.

"I got there but Richardson didn't show up. I stood around. I was tired and mad and lonesome as hell. Finally a civilian came up—I guess he saw something was wrong—and I got to talking to him. He was a very nice guy—vice-president of the club. I told him our story and he said how sorry he was, and asked if he might go to the funeral. He was the first sympathetic person I'd met.

"Presently a truck arrived, driven by a Filipino soldier with a message for me that the funeral had been postponed until ten o'clock tomorrow. This American found out I knew nobody in Cebu, hadn't slept, and had no place to go, so he invited me out to his house for dinner and the night. Before I went, I located our three men who were unwounded. I gave them fifty pesos and told them to go ashore and get drunk and forget the whole mess—if they could.

"Then I went out to this sympathetic American stranger's home, which was on the outskirts on a hill overlooking Cebu City and harbor. I went right to bed after supper, but first I turned on the radio by my bed. It said that Bataan had just fallen. Maybe if they could have been told that those seven fat interisland steamers were on their way loaded with food and quinine, maybe those poor, brave, starved, fever-ridden guys could have held the line a little longer. Well, we in the torpedo boats had done what we could. And I wished that Peggy could know that, and that I could thank her for those two codeine tablets, and tell her how they let Reynolds sit out on the deck and really enjoy his last cigarette.

"Right now Peggy was probably standing in the tunnel entrance on Corregidor, where she and I had sat so many evenings, looking across the narrow waters to the tip of Bataan where the Japs now were, and back up from the water in the hills would be bright pin-points of rifle fire, where the Japs were hunting down like rats those few brave, silly expendables who still wouldn't admit they were expended, who still had a little fight left and so kept on fighting even after the generals had said it was done. Looking at this, probably she was, and knowing that their turn on the Rock would come soon. Well, we in the MTB's were expended now, but we had done what we could for Bataan. And I wished that the swell brave gang on the Rock could know this. Oh, Christ! Oh, Christ! Finally I got to sleep."

"It was a hell of an explosion which woke me up in the dark, and for a minute I didn't know where I was. Through my window which overlooked the town and the harbor beyond, I could see a fire rising on the outskirts. I looked at my wrist watch. It was 4:25. They were all awake in the house now. Then came an even bigger explosion and a flame ten times as high. My American host came back from the telephone and said that one was the Philippine Refinery; the Japanese were coming and the Americans were blowing up the town. I hustled into my clothes and tried to get back into the city. I wanted to rejoin my three men, but I was stopped on the road by the army—no traffic, everybody must get out. It was 5:30, and by now one-third of the city was in flames.

"People were streaming out—some Americans, and a few of our navy. From them during the morning I heard that the Japs had come back and bombed what was left of our 34 boat on the beach. Well, that was over.

"Then I heard that Bulkeley wasn't dead—his boat escaped and was in Mindanao. That Brantingham had burned his 35 boat sitting there on 'Dad' Cleland's marine railway—at least the Japs wouldn't get it. That Ensign Richardson had assembled what was left of our men, and joined up with our naval forces on Mactan Island, where they would all try to escape to the island of Leyte. It was the last I ever heard of them.

"The Japs had already landed twenty miles down the coast of Cebu—also at two other points.

" 'Well, what can I do?' I asked the army.

" 'Nothing,' they said. 'Maybe you'd like to join the other évacués who are assembling at Camp X'—an army stronghold inland which was going to hold out all through the war until help came from the States.

"I couldn't make up my mind, so I waited at this American's house for something better to turn up, and meanwhile watched the Jap invasion from the second-story windows.

"It was on a penny-ante scale—we could have stopped them if we'd had anything at all. They had a destroyer, two transports, and a couple of inter-island steamers not a hundred feet long. This gang lay off the channel entrance for a while, and presently they loaded about a thousand infantry into the two steamers (five hundred in each), which set out in column through the channel. The leading boat had a little 3-inch gun on its bow, and every now and then it would bang away toward the city.

"I watched them tie up at about ten o'clock in the morning at the only remaining dock and disembark. Meanwhile the three seaplanes (yes, the same ones) were flying over the city, dropping leaflets in English telling the Philippines to surren-

183

der, 'We are your friend,' and offering a *substan-
tial* reward for any American, dead or alive, and a
handsome reward for any American officer or his
body. Nice guys. Meanwhile two Zero fighters
were strafing the automobiles trying to get out on
the road.

"Then we got reports on the progress of the
street fighting, which we could also hear from the
house. The general had apparently pulled out—
maybe to fortify Camp X—but the colonel was
staying behind with his soldiers to hold out as long
as he could. He had less than a thousand Filipino
troops, and less than a hundred rounds of ammunition per man. But they would fight until this was
expended. At two o'clock they seemed to be holding their own, and when I shoved off about 2:30
o'clock, half the town was in flames—it was the
second city in the islands—and all the warehouses
were blown up. The Japs later hollered around
about typical American vandalism, but it was one
of the best jobs I saw the army do.

"Meanwhile I had been asking the army what
was so good about Camp X. Well, it was way up
in the hills, they said. It would take days of walk-

ing over footpaths, because all the roads into it were blown up.

" 'But won't the Japs come after you?'

" 'Oh, they'd never do that—it's too hard to get to.'

"What about equipment and guns? Well, they had a radio station, food for several months, a few hundred troops and a few rifles. The more I heard about Camp X, the more distrustful I got, and meanwhile a report came in that the Japs had landed at Toledo. I looked at my map—it was the standard map the army used for operations, put out by the Standard Oil Company with all their filling stations marked—and saw that a good road led directly from Toledo to Camp X. So I asked the army why the Japs wouldn't use it.

" 'Oh, we're going to blow that up, just like the others.'

"But the whole Camp X plan looked lousy to me. I was for last-ditch resistance, but here I was, a lone sailor with no trigger finger (the wound had healed but the joint wouldn't bend any more, so it would be no use in this kind of fighting).

"So I started off by myself for the other coast,

hoping I could get out to some other island where the Japs hadn't come yet. I joined up with some civilians who were going the same way—they were plantation owners and could speak the dialect. It was a forty-two-mile hike over steep trails which crossed five mountain ranges. We carried a few cans of corned beef, and at night would sleep in native huts with pigs and chickens under us and flies over us, and we would get the natives to cook us rice and corn, and buy chickens which they would roast for us. We used banana leaves for plates, and pieces of bark for forks.

"The second day we heard planes at dawn and all scrambled back out of sight in the hut—peering up through the palms. It was three bombers in formation at about fifteen hundred feet.

"Somebody said, pointing, 'Why, look—they're ours!' But I could hardly believe it—even when I saw the stars on their wings, even when I heard the faraway rumble of their bombs dropping on the Japs in Cebu. They were the first American bombers we had seen since before the start of the war. Then we heard some more planes—looked up, and again they were American, a new type with a split tail I'd never seen before but which I learned later were B-25's, and now I realized that here was our big American offensive—the one which we thought had pooped out on us the morning after we sunk the cruiser. Here it was at last—three days too late! Because in the meantime Bataan had fallen, and Cebu, and all they could do now was pester the Japs and sink a few empty transports. I was sore as hell.

"Because we little guys—the ones who are ex- pended—never get to see the broad picture of the war, never find out the reasons back of the moves or failures to move. We only see our part—look up through the palm trees at the seamy side of it. So when something poops out, and help doesn't come, and everything goes to hell, we can only hope help didn't come in time for some sensible reason like bad weather conditions in Australia. We hope, but at the time we can't be sure, and we get mad.

"That afternoon we bumped into a bunch of troops; they had come from Camp X. It seemed that at three o'clock in the morning a sentry heard a noise, called out 'Halt!' and was answered by Jap tank fire. Somebody hadn't gotten around to blow-

187

ing up that road from Toledo. So now impregnable Camp X was no more, all American forces on the island were routed, and everything was going to pot.

"Finally we hit a little native village on the coast and started looking for boats, but the mayor said there were none—the native troops had used them to evacuate that day. But they were swell to us—always out in the country they were swell to us—ignorant guys, maybe, but nice and kind as they could be. I remember on the trail we overtook a ramshackle cart and a few natives, and an old native woman gave the cart driver hell for not putting the baggage in his cart—said we Americans were fighting for their people and they should help us.

"The driver tried to pile it on, but it broke his cart down. He wouldn't take any money—just said he was sorry he couldn't help us more. In those days in the jungle I learned more about how nice the simple Filipino people are than I'd learned in months in Manila; I also learned the more Americanized they are, the lousier they are.

"Leaving this village, we kept on down the road

to an even tinier one on the coast—still looking for boats. We found a military headquarters and a Filipino third lieutenant—just a kid—in command of twenty native troops, no machine guns and almost no ammunition. Ten miles of hard-surfaced road connected it with a town where the Japs had landed. He said a Jap tank had come up the road the first day but had turned around and gone back. Why hadn't he blown up the bridges? No dynamite. What was he going to do if the Jap tanks came again? What could he do, he asked, but evacuate? I noticed they had all their gear packed into a bus, and that under their uniforms they wore their civilian clothing. And I couldn't blame them. But they helped us comb the place for boats, and we finally located enough bancas to carry us, and shoved off at dusk.

"We arrived at the next island soaking wet but thankful, and glad we were halted on the beach by native volunteer guards with home-made rifles, instead of by the Japs.

"Here I said good-by to the American civilians. They owned sugar and coconut plantations and wanted to get to their families. Then they would try to get them to safety, but where was safety? Or maybe, instead of wandering from island to island, it would be better to wait for the Japs in their homes. They couldn't decide. The whole easy, comfortable American world was cracking up fast in those islands. It wasn't nice to watch.

"Meanwhile I caught a ride in a car to the island's military headquarters where there was a general in command, and told the army lieutenant at the desk there that I wanted to get over to the island beyond, provided the Japanese hadn't already taken it—what did he know?

"Well, he said, he didn't know for sure, but he didn't think the Japs had taken it.

"I asked him when he had last communicated with military headquarters over there.

"About a month ago, he said.

"Well, I said, this was urgent—I *had* to find out quick—wasn't there *any* way of getting in communication with them?

"Well, he said, he guessed he *could* pick up the telephone on his desk and call them. But, he explained, I was new around here and didn't understand the local situation. It seemed that his general and the general over on the other island didn't get on at all—hadn't liked each other since West Point. 'You fellows may think you're fighting the Japanese,' he said, 'but here we know better. The front-line trenches of the real war are between these two generals.' However, he said, my case made it different, and since I was a naval officer and therefore, so to speak, a neutral, he thought he could take it on his own responsibility to call up headquarters on the other island and ask in my behalf if the Japanese had landed yet.

"He rang them up, and then reported that at the other end of the wire they were talking something which wasn't English or Spanish. Maybe it was Tagalog, which he didn't speak himself, but just in case it was Japanese I had probably better find some other way of going to Mindanao.

"How the war between the generals came out I never learned; maybe they're finishing it in a Japanese prison camp.

"It took me days to get to Mindanao around through the islands begging rides in cars, hiring small boats to cross little island channels. My objective was to join Bulkeley, who, they had said in

Cebu, had escaped the destroyer and was in Mindanao. I wanted to make my report of my part of the battle to him as commander of our squadron. General Sharp, who commanded the island, surely could tell me where he was.

"A Chinese mestizo who was doing a smuggling business of luxury articles among the islands finally landed me, for an enormous price in pesos, at a tiny village on Mindanao which had been abandoned by everybody but one old man, who said yes, a torpedo boat had been in there the week before, and with gestures drew a pretty good picture of Bulkeley's black beard. But he said they'd been there only a few hours, and left for he knew not where. Then he asked when the Japs were coming. Because all the villagers had left, because they were afraid they'd be killed, but I didn't think the Japs would kill an old man, did I?

"I hopped a ride on a truck on down to Iligan, and there was Bulkeley's 41 boat, tied to the dock!

"The first person I saw was Ensign Cox here, and his mouth dropped open. After a few seconds he said, 'Good God! I heard you were dead!' One by one the crew would come up, stare, then step up to shake my hand and say, 'Gee, Mr. Kelly, we're glad to see you!' "

"After Cebu fell," explained Cox, "an army aviator arrived—he'd left Cebu that morning. He said he'd talked to a Catholic priest who had said burial mass over you and another sailor, killed in an engagement."

"And I was very glad to hear it," said Kelly. "Because then I knew that Harris and Reynolds had gotten decent burial at the American cemetery in Cebu before the Japs arrived. But then I asked, 'Where's Bulkeley?' You see, the last I saw of him he was tearing around the other side of that Japanese cruiser, trying to draw its fire away from me, so I could get in to polish it off. I thought they'd probably got him. I heard he'd turned up later in Mindanao, but it was just a rumor."

"What actually happened was this," said Bulkeley. "They didn't get me, but three destroyers chased me until dawn, when I pulled away into shallow water, and we tied up under a pier to get some sleep—as I think I said.

"When night came I went on up to Iligan, where I intended to get gas and go on up to Cebu to see

193

what had happened to Kelly, although I was pretty sure he hadn't got out alive. But at Iligan I was met by a radioed order from Wainwright; there were no more torpedoes for the MTB's, so he couldn't let us have any gas. They were needing it all for the planes out to Australia.

"So there we were—stuck at Iligan. I went on over to headquarters at Del Monte to report the battle with the cruiser to General Sharp—certain that the end was before us on the island. We'd be fighting here on Mindanao with rifles to the end. But that morning—it was April 13—General Sharp called me in to say he'd just got orders from Melbourne that I was ordered to report to Mac-Arthur immediately on the plane leaving Del Monte that night. For a while I felt rotten. It would look like I was walking out on the squadron. It was an order, of course, but you could tell them to go to hell, and there would be nothing they could do about it, because pretty soon we were going to be killed or captured by the Japanese.

"Then I figured it another way. If I could get to Australia, I might be able to persuade Mac-

Arthur to bring out the rest of the squadron. It looked like it was their only chance. 'I'm going to try to get out all your officers and key men,' he had said. 'I'm not going to let you die in a fox hole with a rifle.' I knew he had believed the MTB's had a great future in the war.

"So I sent word to the rest I would get them flown out if possible, and got aboard the bomber that night. As we left the field, the Japs dive-bombed it and put one motor out, but we got through."

"He left me in charge," said Akers, "and presently General Sharp sent me up to Lake Lanao in the middle of Mindanao Island on a peculiar mission. They were afraid the Japs might land seaplanes on it and I was to set up defenses there. I was to teach the army how to run the machine guns. The lake is about twenty miles long and fifteen wide in the middle of the Moro country. They were planning to take the 41 boat up there when I left. All her torpedoes were gone, but her machine guns were intact, and they wanted to use her as a lake gunboat to keep the place clear of Jap seaplanes so that our flying boats in from Australia would have a place to set down as long as they dared come in. They defended Lake Lanao to the last, and I wouldn't be surprised to learn that the old 41 boat, the flagship of the squadron, fired the last shot of the war out on that lake, protecting the life line to home."

"Cox told me Bulkeley had gone home," said Kelly, "and, thinking I was dead, had made him squadron commander. And I didn't know what to do. There I was—no crew, no boat, no job, while they were busy dismantling the 41 boat, to take it up to Lake Lanao and end the war fighting with the Moros. So I decided I'd better get up to Del Monte and report to Sharp so he could tell Bulkeley I was alive, and send in my report by radio to the States on the scrap with the cruiser and what happened to my boat.

"The General was amazed to see me. 'Bulkeley said you'd been killed in action,' he said. He listened to my report on the battle. 'I'll send you to Kalasungay,' he said, 'near the airfield where the planes come in. But I warn you, there's not too much hope of getting out. There's almost no more gas to refuel the planes at this end, so I doubt that they'll send any more.' I said I was sure we were getting out—MacArthur had told Bulkeley he would do it if it was humanly possible.

"The town was forty-five miles away, and I reported to the army colonel there at noon. He asked me why I was here. 'Waiting transportation to Australia,' I said.

" 'No use getting your hopes up,' he said. 'And since I've had no instructions, I assume you're here on a duty status and am going to put you to work.'

" 'That's okay,' I said, 'if I don't have to leave the vicinity.'

" 'I can't even guarantee that,' he said. 'I'm organizing a carabao pack train to Lake Lanao. They're cutting the trail now. I have another man rounding up fifty carabao and drivers. When he gets them, you'll be in charge of leading the pack train.'

"I didn't say much. I figured he and I were in for a showdown. I didn't intend to miss a plane being off herding a bunch of milk cows through a jungle, but I thought there was no use being unreasonable now. After all, fifty carabao was a lot to round up. It would take several days.

197

"Back at the quarters I found an old navy captain who'd arrived the day before—used to be in
charge of the industrial department at Cavite. He
listened to my story, and MacArthur's promise,
and then said, 'The way it looks, I don't think I'm
getting out.' Then he talked about the thirty years
he'd spent in the navy, all of them training so he
would be useful in case of war, and you could see
it was discouraging for him to end like this—apparently forgotten by the country he had wanted to
serve. What had his life been for?

"He warned me not to count on it—'There
aren't enough planes and gas to take us all.' He was
discouraged himself, and for the next six days the
old man talked it all the time—we are not getting
out, can't get out, won't get out. I suppose he was
afraid to get his own feeble hopes up.

"On the night of April 22 my hopes were
down. I was fiddling with the radio and cut in on
a news broadcast from the States—a short-wave station in San Francisco. It was the navy news release
on our fight with the cruiser! I listened to the story
of how my boat had been forced ashore by the
strafing, and then started wondering what my fam-

ily would think. That night the news commentators in the States had us all winning the war, their buoyant cheerful voices talking of victory. It made me very sore. We were out here where we could see these victories. There were plenty of them. They were all Japanese. I didn't know it would be worse when I got back in the States. Here the enemy have been marching steadily on in every hemisphere, taking more territory and more islands, and yet if even at one point we are able to check or repulse an attack, the silly headlines chatter of a victory.

"I went to bed sick as the silky-voiced commentator again repeated his account of our victory, when all out here knew we had only expended ourselves in the hope that it might slow down a Japanese victory, and we had failed even in this.

"Next morning the army colonel sent for me. He'd had a planeless aviator hard at work who had collected thirty-nine of the fifty carabao. Soon the others would be here, so I was to start work today—a trail-blazing expedition to inspect the jungle path up to Lake Lanao. But suppose a plane came while I was away? I didn't even bring it up;

it seemed so hopeless now. I went back to my quarters and had just packed to go when the phone rang. I was to report to General Sharp at the landing field at once, and bring everything I had with me.

"The old navy captain who shared my quarters knew what that meant. 'Good luck, Kelly! You were right,' he said. There were tears in his eyes, and I could see why. He'd devoted his life to his country, and yet here at the end, in spite of his rank and those years, it wasn't enough.

"What they needed outside now was technicians in the new weapons, and that meant young fellows like me. So now, in spite of the many things he was able and trained to do, and wanted to do, they weren't quite enough, so he was to stay and die in a fox hole or be captured. I said what I could, but it wasn't much, because the old man already knew.

"It was grim waiting at the airport. The priority list was made up in Melbourne and each man had a number. A plane would not hold more than thirty, they knew, but more than a hundred were waiting there. Because perhaps two, maybe even three, planes *might* come. Or perhaps someone whose name was called would not show up, and your number might be high enough on the list to claim his seat. So they waited—all young technicians, most of them aviators, for this last chance to get out, so they could fight again. General Sharp had told me he had telephoned Cox and Akers that they were on tonight's list; why weren't they here?

"Suddenly I saw a familiar face—it was Ohio, the fighter pilot who had been next to my cot in Corregidor. When he left the hospital, of course there was no plane for him, so he'd been an infantry soldier on Bataan. He'd missed this plane here once—his name had been called and he wasn't there. He was hoping it would be called again tonight. After Bataan fell he'd flown twice to Corregidor in that ramshackle old Beechcraft which was about all the air force we had left in the islands now—with medical supplies for our hospital down under the Rock. I asked him about Peggy, and of course he remembered her—the pretty one with green eyes?—sure. But he hadn't seen any of the nurses. He'd had to come in at night while they marked the four corners of the landing field for him with flashlights, and get away as fast as he could. On the last trip he'd bent his propeller landing, and sweated blood while they straightened it for him in the machine shop down under the Rock.

"He stopped here, and a silence of death fell over everybody, for we could now hear motors far above. How many planes? We peered up through the moonlight—now we could see her, and there was only one, circling the field. Lower she came— My God, would she crack up on landing? None of us breathed as her searchlight stabbed for the ground. She was down now, but suppose there was some mistake, and our names weren't on her list? Or suppose while she sat there, gassing, the Japs came over and blew her wings off? And where, I wondered, were Cox and Akers? It was a forty-mile trip for them; had they caught a ride?

"At 10:30 the list was called—thirty names, mine and theirs among them, but only I answered present. So they put an army tank major and an air-corps captain in as substitutes, if they failed to arrive. But at 10:35 here they came on the run, so the captain and the major were turned aside. They were to go on the next plane—if there was a next.

"Just before we got aboard, General Sharp came

over to tell me good-by. He is a grand old man, all six feet of him, a commanding person and every inch a soldier, as his father and grandfather were before him. He'd served two years in the ranks, was a colonel in the last war, and was now a major general.

"He said this was probably the last plane out, and he wanted me to take a message to MacArthur. 'Tell him that the end here is drawing near, and if help can't be sent, in a few days Mindanao will fall. Of course, probably he understands this, and maybe nothing can be done. But,' he said, 'if he asks what we need to hold out, tell him if we had a navy tank force—bringing up a tanker loaded with gasoline and a hundred thousand men, tell him to give me only that and we can hold here, and start taking back the islands.'

" 'I know probably he hasn't got them, but tell him that if he asks.' He was a grand old gent. He knew what he was saying was useless, but he couldn't quite down the hope that maybe they would get a chance to fight on.

"Then he talked about us. 'Everybody left here in the islands should realize,' he said, 'that those who are called to Australia are the ones who will be most useful for the work ahead. Those who leave are the men for the job, regardless of rank and years of service. The rest of us,' he said, 'consider ourselves as being expendable, which is something that may come to any soldier. We are ready for it, and I think they will see that we will meet it squarely when it comes.'

"Then they called my name, we shook hands, and I climbed aboard. Each of us who were leaving unstrapped our 45's and handed them out through the plane's windows to the fellows who were staying behind. They'd be needing them badly and we wouldn't."

"And Peggy?" someone asked.

"There were three seaplanes sent out from Australia to Corregidor at the very last," said Kelly, "which, among other people, were to bring out the nurses. One of them was shot down off Corregidor, but the other two loaded and got back to Lake Lanao, where they gassed up for the big homeward hop while Sharp held the Japs back from the lake. One of these two got safely away; the plane Peggy was in cracked up on the take-off. So now we won't ever know. Maybe she's a prisoner; maybe she's back up in the hills with a few who are still fighting on.

"But as our big ferry-command bomber swung wide out over the field after the take-off, you could see the island and then the path of moonlight glistening over the water, just as we used to watch it glisten from the tunnel entrance at Corregidor. And suddenly I remembered the last thing she said to me—her voice was just as clear as if it had been two seconds ago, instead of many weeks, over that signal-corps telephone in the army hut on Bataan, after I had told her this was good-by. 'Well,' she said, 'it's been awfully nice, hasn't it?' And her voice had sounded clear and brave, but seemed to come from far away."

Officers and Enlisted Personnel Attached to Motor Torpedo Boat Squadron Three

NAME	ADDRESS
John D. Bulkeley	Long Island City, N. Y.
Robert B. Kelly	New York City, N. Y.
Edward G. DeLong	Santa Cruz, Calif.
Vincent E. Schumacher	Kalamazoo, Mich.
Henry J. Brantingham	Fayetteville, Ark.
Anthony B. Akers	Beverly Hills, Calif.
Bond Murray	Dansville, Ga.
George E. Cox, Jr.	Watertown, N. Y.
William H. Plant	Long Beach, Calif.
Cone H. Johnson	St. Joseph, Mo.
Iliff D. Richardson	Los Angeles, Calif.
John X. Balog	Stamford, Conn.
George F. Bartlett	Walnut Grove, Calif.
Clayton N. Beliveau	Lebanon, N. H.
Joseph L. Boudolf	Charleston, S. C.
Ralph E. Brendlinger	Exeter, Mo.
Rudolph Ballough	Norwood, Mass.
William R. Dean	Ogden, Utah
Charles Dimaio	Morris Cove, Conn.
Paul E. Eichelberger	Shippensburg, Penna.
Howard R. Fisher	St. Louis, Mo.
Clemente Gelito	I Bajay, Capiz, P. I.
Floyd R. Giaccani	San Francisco, Calif.
John Shambora	Bethlehem, Penna.

NAME	ADDRESS
George W. Shepard, Jr.	St. Louis, Mo.
Watson S. Sims	Ellabell, Ga.
Doyle J. Smart	Campbell, Mo.
William A. Stambaugh	San Diego, Calif.
Densil C. Stroud	Cleveland Hts., Ohio
John L. Tuggle	Lynchburg, Va.
Arthur D. Waters	Madera, Calif.
Serafin Gines	Alaminos, Pangasinan, P. I.
David Goodman	Brooklyn, N. Y.
Herbert W. Grizzard	Nashville, Tenn.
DeWitt L. Glover	Stockton, Calif.
Dale Guyot	Arcola, Ill.
Morris W. Hancock	Southport, Ind.
John L. Houlihan, Jr.	Chicopee Falls, Mass.
David W. Harris	Richmond, Va.
Velt F. Hunter	Pedmont, Calif.
Paul A. Owen	Bessemer, Ala.
Ernest E. Pierson	Aripeka, Fla.
William H. Posey	Bradenton, Fla.
Richard A. Regan	Upper Darby, Penna.
Willard J. Reynolds	Brooklyn, N. Y.
Carl C. Richardson	Newcastle, Texas
Henry C. Rooke	Atlanta, Ga.
Albert P. Ross	Topsfield, Maine
Robert B. Burnett	Charlotte, Mich.
Robert N. Caudell	Los Angeles, Calif.
Joseph C. Chalker	Texarkana, Texas

NAME	ADDRESS
Ned M. Cobb	Mathis, Texas
Leroy G. Conn	Milton, N. Y.
William E. Cook	Davenport, Iowa
James D. Culp	Denver, Colo.
Marvin H. Devries	Passaic, N. J.
James A. McEvoy, Jr.	Methuen, Mass.
Hayward K. Miller	Wichita, Kan.
Robert H. Monroe	Monterey, Calif.
Edward R. Morey	Medford, Mass.
Theodore L. Morgan	Rome, Ga.
Francis J. Napolillo, Jr.	Baltimore, Md.
Otis F. Noel	Bostonia, Calif.
Ellwood H. Offret	Park City, Utah
Severo Orate	Labrador, Pangasinan, P. I.
Harry G. Keath	Lancaster, Penna.
William F. Konko	Cleveland, Ohio
Robert L. Langer	So. Chicago, Ill.
Clem L. Langston	Birmingham, Ala.
John Lawless	Norfolk, Va.
John H. Lewis	Mt. Holly, Ark.
Benjamin Licodo	Rosales, Pangasinan, P. I.
James D. Light	Vallejo, Calif.
John Martino	Waterbury, Conn.
Stewart Willever, Jr.	Phillipsburg, Penna.
George W. Winget	Oxford, N. J.
Charles C. Beckner	Princeton, Ind.
John W. Clift, Jr.	Wanchese, N. C.